Body Language Secrets

Read the Signals and Find Love,
Wealth and Happiness

Susan Quilliam

Thorsons
An Imprint of HarperCollins*Publishers*

To Desmond Morris – who else?

Thorsons
An Imprint of HarperCollinsPublishers
77–85 Fulham Palace Road,
Hammersmith, London W6 8JB

Originally published in separate volumes as *Optimum Performance*,
Success at Work, *Successful Social Life*, *Making Love Work* and *Total Strangers*
by Thorsons 1996
Published by Thorsons 1997
10 9 8 7 6

© Transformation Management 1996, 1997

Susan Quilliam asserts the moral right to
be identified as the author of this work

A catalogue record for this book
is available from the British Library

ISBN 0 7225 3533 3

Printed and bound in Great Britain by
Omnia Books Ltd, Glasgow

Contents

Acknowledgements

I would first like to acknowledge the many sources and individuals who helped me gain my research material, particularly the staff of the Open University Library, the staff of the University of London Library, and Felicity Sinclair. A special acknowledgement to Samantha Smeraglia for her ability to collate my research so wonderfully!

My thanks also to: Barbara Levy, my agent, for her continued support; Sharon Scotland, the illustrator; to Jane Graham-Maw, Wanda Whiteley, Michele Turney, Jenni Maas, Barbara Vesey and Natalia Link from Thorsons for making the writing and production of this book such an enjoyable experience; to my personal assistant June Bulley for her constant administrative excellence.

And thank you to my husband Ian who, as always, makes all things possible.

Throughout this book, the people referred to could be either 'he' or 'she'. Consistently referring to one gender would not only raise political issues, but would be unfair to the 'other kind'! In general, therefore, unless to do otherwise would make the text inaccurate, I have alternated pronouns in successive questions in this book, to give a balanced feel.

Preface

Before you read this book, remember that body language:

- is every kind of human behaviour *except* the words spoken – from gestures to breathing, from the way muscles move to a person's use of time
- is not able to tell you everything – you may need the words too
- does not let you read everyone like a book – because everyone has his or her own personalized body language
- will not give you power over people – they will not respond unless they want to
- will not work if you try to change others – you can only ever shift what *you* do and alter the situation that way
- is about gathering information – you will be more successful if you do
- is something you already know – your natural body language works best
- is best tried out slowly and carefully – new body language patterns can look false
- works by trial and error: do more of what succeeds, and stop doing anything that doesn't!

1 ♥ Optimum Performance

How Can Body Language Help Me Perform Better in My Life?

Body language is the foundation of personal performance. This is something we have realized only in the last few years, when psychologists have begun to understand the essential links between mind and body. For the way you use nonverbal communication reflects and affects the way you approach things in every area of your life.

Reading your own body language lets you understand your own mental and emotional tactics. You can start to interpret the way you think, how you remember, how you learn. You can begin to analyse your own emotions, when you feel them, how you feel them – and what use they are to you. You can begin to trace how your body language reflects your personality – and how that affects the way people react to you.

You can also start to work *with* rather than *against* your own nonverbal patterns. And, doing so, you can often increase your effectiveness in a whole range of areas. Rather than simply ignoring or pushing down the signals from outside and inside your body, you can start to listen to those signals and use what they are telling you. Rather than getting annoyed when, for example, you are performing below par, you can let your body tell you how to solve the problem.

Also, body language can actually help you change. For one of the most exciting recent developments in psychology suggests that if, in certain situations, we alter our body language, we can also alter our attitudes, perceptions and emotions. It is true that where our minds go, our bodies can often follow; if we decide to do something, then our bodies will rise to the challenge. And it is also true that where our bodies go, our minds can often follow, and that if we act, then our thoughts and feelings will often fall into place too.

If you want to be really effective in life, you have to be aware of body language – and use it.

Does My Natural Physical Appearance Affect the Way People Relate to Me?

The answer to this question is a definite yes. Human beings are influenced by appearance; children as young as two or three months old consistently look, gurgle and smile at photos of some faces more than others.

So what particular elements influence most? Being tall and slim will influence people in your favour; they are likely to judge you as more competent and more attractive. If you are male, being too thin may mean you are seen as a wimp, while fat people of both genders are judged as lazy and self-indulgent.

Do you seem 'all woman' or 'all man'? Very obvious gender signals, such as big breasts and buttocks on a female, or wide shoulders and small buttocks on a male, can make you seem more alluring in situations where sexual attraction is important, such as at a disco. Where sex is not as relevant, though, such as at work, such features can make people mistrust you, judge you as less intelligent, or think you are 'only after one thing'.

When it comes to the shape of your face, the more 'babyish' your face looks the more people will warm to you. Recent research at the University of St Andrews has shown that so-called 'infantile signals' – small nose, full lips, huge eyes, small chin and high cheekbones – stir up people's protective instincts. But these signals may also mean that people do not take you seriously. More mature features, such as a large nose or a prominent jaw, may well make people see you as more of an equal, and be more impressed by what you say or do – even if they do not feel quite so friendly towards you.

Colouring also counts. Sadly, skin colour makes you likely to be stereotyped, sometimes making people prejudge how intelligent you are, how likely you are to succeed in career terms – or how likely you are to break the law! Hair colour can also be seen as reflection of personality: blondes of both genders are seen both as 'more fun' and less intelligent, while redheads are traditionally thought to have fiery tempers, and brunettes to be serious and introverted.

Grey hair can be seen as a sign of distinguished elegance in men, though because it shows that a woman is old enough to be past her childbearing years, it is regarded as less appealing in a woman. (Hence an abundance of 'grey hair colouring' products for women currently on the market in Britain, against only one equivalent product for men!)

All this can seem very depressing. People make an initial judgement in the first ten seconds of meeting you – and base that judgement on your appearance. And it may seem as if you cannot argue with that.

In fact, things are not as bad as they seem. Not only can some parts of 'natural' appearance be shifted – through exercise, careful dressing and 'the appliance of science'. Research has also shown that when people see the wider range of body language that expresses your personality, they can very easily revise their initial judgment. Given ten hours instead of ten seconds, you can influence and attract, whatever your natural appearance.

How Can I Dress for Success?

What kind of success do you want? Everything you wear – clothes, hairstyle, jewellery, accessories – makes a nonverbal statement about your income, your status, your occupation, your personality, your age and your motives. But whether these statements mean that you succeed or fail depends very much on what game you want to play.

Do you want to dress for success at work? Then you need to discover what the 'career uniform' is. This does not only mean following the rules in professions such as the army where an actual uniform is worn. What it means is being aware of the style that has spontaneously developed within your company. Are suits in? Are perms out? How brightly coloured are the ties people wear? Because human beings feel more comfortable with others who 'copy' rather than buck the trend, following the company style consensus may mean all the difference between being simply tolerated and actively promoted. This is discussed in more detail on page 45.

Do you want to make friends? Ask first who these friends are and then what statement they make about themselves by what they wear. If the statement is 'income' or 'status', then you may need to dress expensively. But if your friends are those who do not have wealth or who do not value it, success may well be down to the creative and quirky use of low-cost materials. And if the people you mix with like to be seen as 'practical', spending more time on their families than on fashion, for example, then to be accepted you may have to wear down-to-earth rather than stylish clothes.

Success in love is often thought to depend on dressing sexily. Men, for example, tend to believe that if people dress to show off the more sexual parts of their anatomy, then what they want is sex. But this is not necessarily true for women, who may dress sexily to feel attractive, and sometimes to score points off their female rivals – but very rarely to signal that they simply want sex.

In fact, success guidelines in this context are these: To attract a partner initially, wear what gets his or her attention – that way, you are more likely to make contact and get talking. Women tend to be attracted to people who are fashionable and colour-co-ordinated, while men notice strong colours, the use of make-up and shape-enhancing styles. Once you have attracted your partner, and got to know him or her, then choose your clothes first to reflect those parts of your personality that he or she particularly likes – your sense of fun, your elegance, your practicality – and secondly to encourage your partner literally to keep in contact with you because you wear sensuous, touchable clothes!

The bottom line, with all dress decisions, is to fit the time, the place, the context and the people. The more you understand about whomever you are dressing to impress – and the more you use that understanding to customize what you wear – the more successful you will be.

How Does My Environment Reflect What I Am Like as a Person?

If your environment truly reflects you – in other words, if you have actually chosen what is in it – then it will show other people a great deal about you.

For example, how introverted or extroverted are you? Studies show that physiologically, extroverts are better able to cope with sensory stimulation than are introverts. It is likely, then, that if you are the former you will fill your environment with rich colours and patterns and a great deal of detail in design; if you are the latter, you will opt for simple shapes, plain colours, dim lighting. Of course, you may be more or less introverted or extroverted in different situations, so you may allow more colour and detail in the public areas of your life such as the kitchen or the hall, and quieter design in the more private areas such as the bedroom.

Here is another personality distinction: Which of your three major senses is most important to you – sight, hearing or touch? For every human has a preferred sense – one which, almost from the beginning of our lives, is the one that attracts us most. Our preference then influences the way we arrange our environment. If you are a 'visual' person then you are likely to put the emphasis on how things look – as did one top designer who bought his easy chairs solely for their appearance, and realized only after they had been delivered that they were excruciatingly uncomfortable to sit on!

What if you are a person to whom sounds or voices matter most? Your money will go on the stereo system and you may never even get round to repainting the walls or replacing battered or unfashionable furniture. If you are a person to whom touch is vital, then you will spend most time and money on deep, luxurious seating and velvet cushions. In fact, most people combine all three senses in varying amounts and contexts; consider what the balance is for you.

What is the main focus of your environment? If people are the most important thing in your world, then your environment will probably reflect that. The furniture focus will be 'social', with

chairs and sofas turned towards each other; a rou.
where you can easily see people and interact with th.
where you can cuddle up.

What if your space is centred around something neu.   .ups
a log fire? This does not mean that people are unimport..ht to you.
It may mean, however, that you need to focus inside yourself, need
time and space for yourself when you get home. If your focus is
outward, perhaps a chair placed by a window, then you like to
make contact with the outside world; perhaps you do not go out
much during the day, or that even if you do you still see what happens 'out there' as vital.

A final thought: If you feel uneasy in your surroundings it could
be because they do not truly reflect who you are. Try adding elements, or taking them away, using the insights above as a guide-
line. Consciously designing your environment to reflect your
personality can make you feel more at home.

What Do I See in My 'Mind's Eye'?

If you have seen something once, then you can imagine it. Even if
you have never seen something, given a good enough description
or enough similar experiences, you can think of what it would
look like.

When you do this, you use your 'mind's eye'. You conjure up a
picture of what you are thinking about. So if asked to think of your
kitchen at home, then you will almost certainly visualize that
room. Every human being can do this – even if some of us are less
able to remember their mental pictures than are others.

The study of this part of body language – the pictures people
have inside their heads – is a new and very interesting development in the field of psychology. One of the things such study has
shown is that what you see in your mind's eye is never the same as
reality. Even if you think of something you know well, such as
your kitchen sink, you will not see it in your mind's eye as you

uld in real life. In your mind's eye you might see that sink much more vaguely than it really is; perhaps not as brightly coloured; smaller or bigger than in reality. You might see it as full of water, empty of water, stacked with dishes – or with someone standing by it. The same kitchen sink as visualized by different people looks very different.

Fascinatingly, it now seems that these differences are linked to our emotions. We see differently in our mind's eye things that we feel differently about. Everyone has his (or her) own special way of seeing things – but, for example, some people actually flood their mind's eye image with a warm pinkish tinge when they feel very optimistic about something. On the other hand, if pessimistic or depressed, some people 'add' a cold bluish tint to what they imagine. So phrases like 'rose-coloured glasses…I'm feeling blue…' are not just words; they describe the way that some of us, at least, actually visualize things.

It is not only colour that reflects what we feel. Shape, brightness, focus, contrast, movement – all these vary in our mind's eye, and each variation reflects how we think and feel about what we see. Photographers and cameramen know all about this – and often manipulate their images to create feelings in the same way that the human brain does. If we are in love, for example, we often imagine our partner's face as slightly softened; in the same way, wedding photographers will use soft focus for the shot of the bride and groom. If we are scared of people, however small they actually are in real life, we often see them in our mind's eye as looming above us; film-makers copy this when they shoot from below to communicate a feeling of fear to the viewer.

Studying the mind's eye is something new. But already it is beginning to look possible that we can use it to help people in various ways – with phobias, with traumas, with all kinds of personal development issues. Changing the way we see things – through our mind's eye – may well prove to be one of the keys to enabling human beings to live life to the full.

How Do My Gestures Show Me How My Mind Works?

What you think in your mind, you reflect in your gestures. As you talk, so you trace in the air what you experience in your mind's eye and your 'mind's ear' – a 'between the lines' glimpse of what your words are not saying.

Your gestures might reflect reality. You might draw out in the air something you have seen or heard – to communicate it to others. Of course gestures never literally nor accurately depict the size and shape, rhythm, volume or sensation of what you have experienced. But they do show how your mind works on these experiences – they do show how you think about them.

So let's say you use the classic angler's gesture that goes with the words 'it was *that* big'. That gesture does not reveal the actual size of the fish – but it does show the size you would really want it to be.

A series of tense circular hand movements as you describe how your car would not start does not mimic accurately the sound of the failing ignition. But it does reflect both the rhythm of that sound and the frustration you felt when you heard it!

Gestures also reflect more abstract things. You talk about a friendship and curve your hands together tightly. You describe a project you are starting and wave your hands vaguely. You say you are signing contracts on a new house, and slap one fist into the other hand's open palm. Here, you are revealing how you think about concepts – a friendship, a project, a house purchase. And again, the gestures (taken in context) let observers read between the lines. The tight circle shows that you believe you and your friend are close. The unclear shapes show the project that you are working on is vague or undeveloped. The forceful fist gesture shows your excitement about buying a house.

Because everyone's mind works differently, the same gestures have different meanings for different people. But there are some general guidelines that may help you interpret. For instance, the size of your gestures often indicates how important the thing is that you are talking about – a big gesture indicating that something is vital, a small gesture that it is trivial. A moving gesture can show progression – how something is developing or evolving. Speed in a gesture is often linked to positive or negative emotion – slow gestures expressing gentleness or boredom, fast gestures revealing excitement or tension.

Two hands used for the same movement emphasizes what you are talking about – you use both hands to make the point more unmistakably than if you used just one. But each of your hands, acting independently, can also 'act out' elements in what you are saying. The relative position of each hand can then indicate the relationship of the things you are talking about – as in the friendship gesture described earlier.

Where are your gestures positioned around you? A 'high' gesture, above shoulder level, may indicate status, significance or positivity. If your hands touch your body then they are indicating physical or emotional closeness. If they move away from your body, they indicate distance – worry if you catch yourself talking about someone who is supposed to be close to you but find yourself using away-from-the-body gestures!

What shapes do your hands make as they move? Flat, closed hands indicate straight, direct concepts – certainty, concentration, clarity. If moving downwards, they can indicate an ending or a halt; if turned upwards, openness or a question; if pointed forwards, a forward move. Hands with fingers open often reveal uncertainty or vagueness. Finally, hands that are curved, whether apart or together, tend to show positive emotions or ideas – support, affection, closeness, unity, completion.

How Does My Body Help Me Remember Things?

Whenever we experience something, we also store that experience. In other words, we put sights, sounds and feelings into our physiological memory banks, then retrieve these memories. We cannot remember everything we have ever done, because our experience is so vast and because our ability to recall things may fade with time. But we can remember a great deal. You can probably recall, for example, what colour your bathroom is, or how the bath water sounds rushing down the plughole.

And if you remind your body of a past memory, then it will give you that memory back. The images in a photo album will bring back tiny and very specific details of people and places we had long forgotten. A special tune can reduce us to tears because it reminds us of a particular face, a particular voice, a particular kiss. The smell as we enter a tiny, musty grocer's store may take us all the way back to the corner shop we used to visit as children.

Some counsellors go one stage further – they claim that if we place our bodies in positions of particular stress, for example by breathing deeply and rapidly for extended periods, then feelings that have been buried for years will come to the surface. And as we express those emotions – of anger, joy or fear – we may well be able to remember much more clearly the original events that made us feel those emotions, many decades ago. Once again, we are using our bodies directly to stir up old memories.

Recent research by U.S. psychologists Richard Bandler and John Grinder takes a new tack. They suggest that our eyes move in particular ways when we remember particular things. So, for example, if we are remembering something we have seen – a face, a house, a building – in our mind's eye, then we will look up . If we are remembering something we have heard – a sound, a voice – in our mind's ear, then we will look across . And if we are remembering something we have felt – a hug from a friend, a moment of strong emotion – then we will look slightly down. More detail about just how we do this can be found on page 91.

How much can you use any of these methods to help you remember things? It is certainly worth trying all of them: using mementos to help you reminisce over past events, working with a counsellor who specializes in 'bodywork' to retrieve early emotional memories, experimenting with looking in different directions when trying to remember something you have seen or heard. Of course, none of these approaches is guaranteed. But it is beginning to become clear that, using body language as a lever, we may be able to remember far more than we ever thought we could.

How Can I Spell Better?

Are you hopeless with words? If it is true that when you remember things you have seen, your eyes move in a particular way (*see page 92*), then this can help you develop your ability to spell.

Robert Dilts, a student of the original researchers who made the link between memory and eye position, went on to study the body language differences between people who spell well in the English language, and people who do not spell well.

Dilts found some interesting things. When asked to remember a word, the 'good spellers' consistently glanced up and to the left (right for left-handed people). Some of them even lifted their heads, as if to 'get a better view'. And they actually reported being able to 'see' the word they were spelling in their mind's eye – very often in white lettering on a black background, as if they were actually remembering the very chalkboard on which they had first seen the word spelled!

Poor spellers, on the other hand, could not mentally see the word at all. They had no picture in their mind's eye, and just guessed at what the spelling was before finally getting it wrong. They also did not look up, but kept their heads down, looking at the floor while trying to spell.

Dilts tried an unusual experiment – one which he has success-fully repeated with many people since. He asked the poor spellers to look at a word on a piece of paper; then he asked them to try to recall the word while using the body language of good spellers. Amazingly, with a change of posture and eye direction, these peo-ple could often see their chosen word, and spell it correctly – and could repeat that success in future.

Try repeating Dilts' experiment. First, write down a word you know you can spell. Then imagine it on a board, floating above your head and a little to your left (right, if you are left-handed). Can you see the board clearly? Can you see the word on the board? If not, imagine it bigger and brighter, until each letter is obvious. Then 'read' out the word, letter by letter, forwards then backwards – just to be sure you have all the letters in place.

Once you can do this, try putting a more difficult word 'on the board'. Once you are sitting up and looking up, make the word as big and bright as you need to in order to see it. Keep going until you can read the word letter by letter, forwards and backwards. Practise perhaps 20 times, to hammer it home. On the next occa-sion you need to spell that word, use the right body language – sit-ting up and looking up.

Then, whenever you see a word you know you are not sure of, pop it up on your board. Make it big and bright, practise reading it forwards and backwards – until you know that you will get it right in the future.

What Does Body Language Reveal About My Idea of Time?

Everybody has an image in his (or her) mind's eye of how he sees the past or the future. It is developed as you grow, by seeing clocks, calendars, diaries and other ways of 'marking time'. It means that when you are asked what happened on a particular day in the past, you often get a mental representation of it. And if you are asked to imagine what you will be doing on a particular

day in the future, you are often able to visualize the date you are thinking about.

Research carried out in the U.S. suggests that, fascinatingly, most people see this mental image of events in the past and future as actually being in a specific position, in space, in relation to their bodies. The past is usually over to the left or slightly behind us; the future is often over to the right or in front. Past and future are usually 'joined' by an imaginary line, which would seem to run directly through our bodies. In fact, we often reflect what we see in our mind's eye by phrases such as 'I'm putting the past behind me,' 'here and now' or 'the future lies ahead...'

In terms of body language, people actually signal the way they 'see' time – by the way they gesture and the direction in which they look. If, when you think of what happened last Christmas you see that as to your left and slightly behind you, then as you talk about it you will also tend to look back to your left, and make a minute hand-movement in that direction.

If, when you imagine what will happen on your next birthday, you see that as in front of you, then when you talk about your upcoming birthday party your hand-movements will tend to point forward and you will face forward. Not surprisingly, when you discuss the present you are likely to make gestures that indicate the spot you are standing on.

And if you are talking about something that has happened in the past and will go on happening in the future, your gestures and the direction in which you look may well trace your imaginary 'time' line, from past to future, from left to right or from back to front. Your time line will have a particular shape: some time lines are simply straight, others curve or go in waves.

Your time-line shape can also alter according to how you feel about the events on it. So, for example, pay attention if you see yourself tracing a downward sloping time line with your hand as you describe how you see your life developing; you are probably feeling pessimistic about some aspect of it. On the other hand, if you use an upward time-line movement, the chances are that your mood is an optimistic one – you see the future actually stretching …'onwards and upwards…'

How Does My Body Learn Naturally?

Desmond Morris, who first brought nonverbal communication to the attention of the Western world, once wrote that a human being, the naked ape '…is a teaching ape'. Almost more miraculously, however, the naked ape is a learning ape. Unlike most mammals, and far more than our primate cousins, we learn from what we see around us, through imitation.

This ability is innate and instinctive. As early as a few minutes after birth, newborns are able to copy vital survival movements such as opening their mouths (to take food) and sticking out their tongues (to refuse food). And most of us are very well aware that children learn by copying – not only the things we want them to imitate, such as eating with a knife and fork, but also the things we do *not* want them to imitate, like the swear word we hear our three-year-old chanting happily to herself! It is this innate ability to copy which lets children develop so rapidly, and master so many of the complex skills that make them human, such as walking, talking, reading and writing.

As adults, it may seem to us that we do not learn in this way, but we do. Right up to the time we die our bodies imitate what we see around us. We copy the obvious bits of other people's behaviour, such as posture, gesture and facial expression, imitating someone else's nonverbal patterns often within minutes of meeting. You may well have noticed how you 'pick up' a person's accent if you spend time with her (or him). But have you noticed how you copy her way of opening a door, her particular taste in food, her habit of sighing and leaning back in the chair at moments of deep satisfaction?

We also, amazingly, copy what happens to someone physiologically. So if someone we are close to gets irritated and her heart rate rises, her breathing quickens and adrenalin rushes round her body, then we will be similarly affected.

And if we spend a lot of time with this person, living or working with her regularly, then we may well learn to reproduce this reaction in a more generalized way. If something happens that would have irritated her, we will learn to get irritated ourselves – even if she is not in the room. In this way, we even 'learn' illness from other people, developing stomach ulcers, tension headaches or back problems simply because someone we are close to suffers from these conditions.

Happily, we also learn more positive nonverbal approaches. We can pick up other people's sense of humour, their tidiness, their love of nature. And of course, we lend them our talents in return. Because our bodies learn, we give and receive body language strategies every day of our lives.

What Happens When I Cannot Concentrate – and Is There Anything I Can Do About It?

Let's begin by looking at what happens when you *can* concentrate. You focus in on one thing. Your vision narrows, your hearing filters out what is not important. You reflect this in your body language by leaning forwards, staring at what interests you and raising your shoulders as if to block out everything else.

But what if you cannot concentrate? Then the outside world distracts you. One thing or another keeps shifting you away from a concentrated state. You glance around, turn around, get caught up in what you hear and see.

What can you do to concentrate better? If you are aware of the distraction, you can change it. But your body can be distracted by things that you may not be aware of. You may not register that the lighting is too dim, but your body may think it is time for sleep and so lose energy for what you are doing. You may not realize that silence may be distracting you, but too little sound can make your body wonder if something is wrong, and so be on the defensive instead of focused on the job in hand.

The distraction may not be outside, but inside you. There are many body functions that are so vital to survival that they take precedence over everything else. So if you have just eaten and need energy to digest your food, this may come first as far as your body is concerned; hard work after a meal just may not be possible. Equally, studies have shown that if your temperature rises or falls too much, if you are too hungry or thirsty, or if you have not had enough rest, your body will alert you to these potentially threatening conditions and keep on giving you these 'alert' messages until you take action.

And, unfortunately, your body can play tricks on you. If you are tense about doing a task your body may well provide you with an excuse not to do it by distracting you with a signal that seems like a survival issue. You suddenly feel very sleepy or very hungry, even if you are well rested and well fed! If this happens to you, rather than resting or eating try reducing any tension you may feel by stretching and breathing deeply. You may find that your fatigue or hunger has disappeared.

Lastly, give your concentration an extra boost by taking on the right body language. Literally turn your back on any possible distractions and focus your attention on the task in hand. Bend over your desk, hunch your shoulders, make your task the centre of your focus. If your body acts as if it is concentrating, then mysteriously you may soon find that your mind does too!

Does My Body Really Talk to Me?

Unbelievable as it may sound, your body communicates with you on a minute-by-minute basis. It tells you when to take action, when to avoid something, even when to be happy!

Actually, you already know this. You already know that your body communicates with you about survival issues. For example, if you are thirsty your body signals this by giving you a particular sensation in your mouth and throat. If you need sleep then your eyelids droop, your limbs feel heavy and you yawn. If your finger is too close to a candle flame then your body alerts you immediately, with a sharp pain that makes you pull your hand back. These physical sensations, these 'internal' signals, are an unmistakable message from your body that you cannot afford to ignore.

Your internal responses signal much more subtle things, too. They may tell you when you are going to be ill – migraine sufferers often report a 'warning feeling' a few days before the event. These responses may signal when you have made a mistake – as when you have a stomach upset and, mentally checking what might have caused it, you feel a sudden spasm as you think of one particular food. Your internal messages may even tell you what the weather's going to be like – as you will know very well if you are an arthritis sufferer who gets 'twinges' when rain is on the way.

Your body also signals, quite specifically, what your feelings about something are. If you experience any of the many emotions humans are capable of – such as fear, anger, anxiety, excitement, surprise, disgust – then what you experience are actual physical sensations inside your body. So if you are delighted that you have got something you wanted, that feeling of delight might be a light sensation throughout your body and a fluttering movement in your stomach. If you are upset that you have missed out on an opportunity, that feeling of sadness might take the form of a heavy sensation throughout your body and a prickling, tearful sensation in your eyes.

Take seriously the internal language of your body. It can tell you when you may have to be wary – perhaps your gut will churn or your back will tense up. It can tell you when you might have reasons to be optimistic – perhaps you will feel a smile coming on, or an excited rise in your breathing rate. If you start to become aware of the messages that your body is sending you, you will be able to understand situations more fully – because you will have the evidence not only of your eyes and ears, but also of how your body feels inside.

How Do I Tell When I Am Unsure About Something?

It is vital for you to know when you are sure about something and when not. Fascinatingly, human bodies do have a mechanism for expressing this – for telling you when you are uncertain and for signalling to others that you need support because of that uncertainty.

A simplified explanation of what happens is this. When your eyes, ears and other senses experience something and are sure of what they are experiencing, then they send clear messages to the brain via the nervous system. The brain interprets what it sees, and you take action.

'To be or not to be'

But if your senses haven't enough information, or your brain cannot quite interpret that information or the information available is contradictory, then two things happen. First, you are alerted to lack of certainty by signals on the inside. Secondly, you send out signals of your lack of certainty on the outside – just in case you need others to help you.

Because what is happening to your body is focused around the nervous system, you are most likely to be aware of internal signals that are located around the central communication network of your nervous system, the spinal cord. Everyone's signals differ; yours might consist of a sinking feeling in your stomach, an uneasy feeling behind your eyes, a tension around your throat or a fluttering in your breathing. If the information you are working on is contradictory, then your body's signals may actually be different on one side than on the other, making you feel 'unbalanced'.

You will reflect all these internal signals on the outside of your body. You may shift to get rid of the discomfort in your stomach or head. You may rub your chest to ease your breathing. You may look puzzled or frown. If you feel 'unbalanced', you may find yourself shifting from one foot to the other, wiggling your shoulders, shaking your head or twisting your mouth. That verbal statement of uncertainty 'I'm weighing up the options' often has its parallel body language, a 'weighing' movement of the hands that seems to measure one thing against another.

Body language itself cannot make you any more sure of anything than you already are. No one movement or exercise will help if you simply do not have the facts at your fingertips, or if you need support to interpret those facts. Where body language *can* help is when you use it to alert you to your own uncertainty, when its signals hold you back from making a potential mistake in signing the document, making the promise, buying the car.

When you are sure, your nonverbal signals will alter. Your settled stomach, easy breathing, balanced posture, calm breathing or direct gaze will all tell you that, whether or not you are in fact making the correct judgment, you are at least certain about what you think and feel.

How Does My Body React to Danger?

When humans lived physically dangerous lives, those who did not know when to be afraid did not survive very long. So even though we now do not need to be on red alert for most of the day and night, we do react strongly to possible danger. We produce a set of body responses that we call fear – or anxiety, wariness, insecurity. Our bodies signal when something threatens – be it a physical threat such as a car speeding towards us or an emotional threat such as someone disliking us. We register these signals inside our bodies, and then display them on the outside, in order to get help if necessary.

Fear body language is all about escape. Your internal organs get geared up for you to run away: your heart rate speeds up, your blood-pressure rises, your liver floods your body with sugar. These preparations give you energy in order to flee – and also give you the classic symptoms of butterflies in your stomach as adrenalin surges, a cold feeling as blood rushes to support your internal organs, a dry mouth from rapid breathing, sometimes an urgent desire to go to the loo as if to lighten your body for faster movement! These internal signals are your body's way of telling you that there is something happening that you ought to run away from.

In fact, in most normal situations you stand your ground. You do not run away from a job interview, an argument with a friend or a tricky tackle on the sports field. You register the fear but ignore it and carry on regardless because, in reality, these are situations in which you want to succeed. And while you may turn rather pale, shake with nerves or lick your lips to prevent a dry mouth, you will show these responses in such a toned-down way that other people may not even notice them.

There is, however, one common situation in today's world where you not only feel terrified but show all the signals of real panic: horror videos. If, on screen, the door creaks open or the mad axeman strikes, your body reacts almost as it would if these events were really happening. You scream (to summon help), cling on to a friend (for support), flinch away (to protect yourself), kick your feet (as if to run away). Then you collapse in giggles as the adverts come on!

In fact, nowadays, when physical threat is rarely part of day-to-day life, your body may actually enjoy all this. In a strange sort of way, in a situation where you know that you are actually quite safe, giving your body such a thorough internal workout often feels good. Dracula and Frankenstein – thank you!

What Really Happens When I Am Angry – and How Should I Handle That?

When you get angry, you are getting ready to fight. Anger is what is left of the impulse that primitive humans had to attack whomever or whatever seemed to be a threat. So if a friend insults you or you get caught in a traffic jam, your body goes on full alert for the possible battle to come!

On the outside, your body will automatically take on a posture designed to warn off the attacker. So your shoulders may square as if for action, your head and lips may jut forward threateningly, your eyebrows may lower in the aggressive expression that monkeys use as a prelude to attack. And on the inside, your nervous, cardiac, circulatory and respiratory systems gear up for emergency action. What you feel on the inside, as this happens, may well be a rush of energy, an urgent desire to move, to hit out, to attack.

Of course, you will hardly ever really attack. Few situations nowadays lead to a full-scale battle, and it is rarely acceptable to come to blows, however irritated or frustrated you get. So you will try to stifle the anger, push it down and carry on as if nothing has happened.

This sounds good, but it has its drawbacks. Feeling angry is your body's way of telling you to take action – and if you cannot do that then your body is left high and dry, with all its systems ready to act but not acting. The results can, in medical terms, be unfortunate;

your body's responses may lead to diseases such as stomach ulcers, heart attack, depression. So while it is socially harmful to act on your anger, it may be physiologically harmful to your body to ignore that anger completely.

So if you feel angry, first note it. Then try to take the edge off your rage so you do not hit out. Take action – in any harmless way you can. Some people opt for slamming doors and banging down cups – but, more constructively, you could dig the garden, beat some rugs, play a hard game of squash. Clearing your body of the stress of anger will not only help you feel better, it will also make you better able to go back and tackle the problem that made you angry in the first place.

How Do I Use Body Language to Feel Better?

Something bad happens – a chance unkind comment or a real frustration. And though you can cope you are in need of a little comfort. How does your body help?

The first thing you will probably do is instinctively touch yourself. There is sense in this; being touched was the basic way that you were reassured when young. The most usual comfort touches are on the head and hands – where adults pat young children – and so your hand will move to your face, you may lean your cheek on your palm, stroke one hand with the other, or pinch the fleshy part of your thumb.

Or your body may want the comfort of rhythm – another early reassurance signal. So you may 'rock', swaying backwards and forwards in a rhythmic movement that recreates being in the womb or being rocked in someone's arms. You may drum your fingers or feet in a way that imitates the sound of a comforting heartbeat.

You may also try to get comfort from others. Unconsciously your posture may slump, your head may droop and your gestures may become slow and weary almost as if you are so tired that you need to be carried. Your face shape may actually change, so that within

minutes it becomes pinched and thin, or puffy and tired – childhood signs of needing to sleep that in adults signal that they need to be looked after. There is nothing actually wrong with you physically, but your body sends out these signs as the best way it knows to get others to give it some attention and support.

What if there is no help around? You are in public, at work, or in a situation where asking for support just is not possible. Or you realize that the best way to solve the situation is simply to act. Then perhaps you will try to cope, deliberately manipulating your physiology to cheer yourself up. You may straighten your posture – which makes it less likely that you will feel sad. You may breathe deeply in and out, which will relax you. You may tip your head back and look upwards – because this tends to distract your mind from any distressing inner sensations. You may start to move, shaking hands and feet or shifting your body position – aiming to boost your energy to override your bad feeling.

At some point you may try to give yourself the comfort that other people are not giving you. Where possible you reach for a warm sweater, soft blanket or duvet; raising your body temperature helps you feel better because it releases energy that your body would otherwise use trying to keep your vulnerable internal organs warm. You may eat or drink warm, soothing, carbohydrate-filled meals – not only because warm food helps your body fight off fatigue and illness, not only because carbohydrates act as natural sedatives, but also because eating and drinking are part of your body's earliest memories of comfort.

Finally, you will probably opt for a good night's sleep. Sleep heals – so much so that, as described above, the natural response to feeling bad is often to become drowsy. And, given the chance to recover and refresh yourself completely, most things will seem better in the morning.

Is There a Way to Motivate Myself through Body Language?

What happens when you do not feel motivated to do something? It is not that you do not want to do it, nor that you cannot do it. But whenever you try, you get a sinking feeling in your stomach, almost a revulsion. You may feel irritated, so tighten your jaw and tense your shoulders. You may feel simply exhausted, with drooping eyelids and a heaviness in your chest.

From the outside, the body signals will be clear. You may sit heavily in your chair, with no muscle tension. Your eyes may be glazed, your head sunk into your shoulders. You may have your arms crossed in front of your body, as if to create a distance between you and whatever it is you are not motivated to do. Recent research shows that people who are uninterested in what they are hearing often display two clear and consistent nonverbal signals: they lean back and away from the source of what they do not want to hear, and they stretch out their legs in front of them.

Of course, the answer to such clear signs of demotivation may have nothing to do with body language. Perhaps you have been told to get on with a job you feel does not need doing; perhaps you have done the job so often that you are bored; perhaps you fear that you are going to get it wrong. If so, then you probably need to use words to figure out, alone or with other people, how you can think and feel differently about what needs to be done.

But if you simply want to feel more enthusiastic about something, then body language *can* help. The secret is that if your body behaves in a particular way, this often convinces your mind to follow suit. So remember how your body responds when you do feel motivated to do something. Maybe you feel more energetic: your posture may be more upright, your eyes wide open to see better, your head tilted to hear better. If seated, you almost certainly reverse the two key 'demotivation signals' and lean forward, with your legs tucked under you. You move quickly and alertly, to get on with the job. Inside, you feel neither queasy nor weary, but full of vitality, with a kind of 'buzz'.

Once you have identified the body language that you personally use when you are motivated, you need to alter your body language deliberately to that pattern. You will first need to raise your energy level, increasing your heart rate and breathing – because energy is the key to getting your body to feel more positive about the job in hand. You might want to take a short bout of exercise, jumping up and down a few times or running on the spot. Then, once you feel more energetic, allow the rest of your body language to take on a motivated pattern, sitting up, leaning forward, tucking your legs underneath you, opening your eyes slightly wider, moving more quickly.

It may seem as if you are pretending to feel something you don't. But if you use your actions as a kind of 'pump primer' to get your body going, pretty soon you will feel better about the job in hand, and spontaneously you will be better able to feel naturally motivated about it.

What Stages Does My Body Go through When I Am Grieving – and What Happens If I Ignore these Stages?

When you suffer a major loss your body grieves. It responds with a whole series of prolonged nonverbal reactions – but why? These reactions certainly do not bring back the person, relationship or job that you have lost. Instead, your body's responses almost seem to make things worse, incapacitating you as you cry, feel tired, get depressed.

But these body reactions are there for a reason. It is almost as if, having suffered a loss that you actually cannot do anything about, rather than trying to take action, your body is demanding extra support and comfort to make up for that loss. The fact that you are incapacitated forces you to give yourself that extra support, or to allow other people to give it to you, in a way that simply would not happen if you were not feeling so bad.

The initial stage you may go through is shock. Even if for just a few moments or hours, when you first learn that you have suffered a loss you become slightly numb, as if to protect your body

from the stress that will follow when you fully realize what has happened. Then, for a few days or weeks you may go through a phase of being physically vulnerable; getting tired easily, feeling dizzy, suffering from minor illness, loss of appetite or an inability to sleep. These reactions may immobilize you, giving you an excuse to be looked after.

The classic sign of grief is that you cry – although how much you do, and whether in public or private, is likely to depend on what gender you are and your cultural background. But controlling yourself too much can be unwise; tears are the body's way of reducing stress, and contain substances that reduce depression. It may seem 'weak' to weep, but physiologically it is helpful; afterwards your body will be a little better able to cope.

As time passes you may find yourself feeling angry. You may feel angry at the event that caused your loss, at the people responsible, sometimes at whomever or whatever it is that you have lost. This anger is a positive thing; the effect on your body is to give you more energy, making it possible for you to start getting on with your life.

It is tempting to ignore the stages of grief. And, in fact, you may not need to go through every phase. But if you just carry on regardless when your body signals any of these stages, then full recovery is less possible. For the physical impact of loss is very real; studies have shown that following the death of a partner, for example, survivors are less able to fight off illness, more prone to develop cancer, more likely to die of heart disease. So pay attention to what your body needs when you are mourning. For grief can kill; dying of 'a broken heart' is no myth.

How Do I Know How Close to Be to Other People?

Just how close you want to be to people depends on how safe you feel with them. Unless we are in a crowd and have no option, we tend to keep people we do not know outside the 'public zone' of more than 3.6 m (12 ft). People we know only as colleagues or acquaintances can come within our 'social zone' of 3.6 – 1.2 m (12 – 4 ft) – though they may come closer to say hello or goodbye. Within the personal zone of 1.2 m – 45 cm (4 ft – 18 in), we allow family and friends, and only lovers and children are allowed to come closer than 45 cm (18 in), to cuddle up and actually touch.

But these distances are generalized. How close you want to be to others also depends on many other things. It can depend on how you were brought up: those raised in 'touching' families tend to grow up as touchers themselves. It can depend on the sort of culture you come from: one study revealed that in Puerto Rico acquaintances spending an hour together touched 180 times, while the score in Paris was 110 times, in Florida once and in London not at all! How happy you are to be close can even depend on how acceptable the other person's odour is to you: if he (or she)

smells threatening, perhaps because his personal hygiene is poor, then you will unconsciously move back out of range.

How close you get also depends on the mood you are in. If you are upset you may well allow people to come very close and touch you for support. If you are scared, you will pull back from those you are wary of and keep extra close to those you feel can take care of you. At the other end of the extreme, if you are irritated you may keep well away from people so that they do not notice your negative expression or gestures – or so that you do not give way to temptation and lash out at them.

If other people get too close for comfort, your body sounds the alarm bells. You feel strong and often painful inner sensations, a combination of fear and anger that alerts you to danger and then tells you either to run or attack. So you may feel panic in your stomach or a rush of nervous energy that makes you want to protect yourself. You move back, turn away sharply and use angled gestures so that others have to step back – or you may even unconsciously frown and look angry so that people feel wary of you and spontaneously steer clear.

If, on the other hand, you feel you are too far away from someone, then you may also feel bad. If a friend chooses to sit on the opposite side of the room, or a lover chooses to sit at the opposite end of the sofa, you may feel uncomfortable and rejected. You will automatically try to cut down the distance between you – shifting forward, leaning forward or stretching out your hand to bridge the gap.

In body language terms, we spend a great deal of our lives dancing round people. We move forward, edge back, shift sideways, all to get just the right distance between us. Only when we get that balance of closeness and separation can we settle down and concentrate on interacting happily, person to person.

How Can I Develop My Leadership Potential?

Whatever the situation – guiding a group of friends to a restaurant or taking a sports team to victory – leading a group is more challenging than simply interacting one-to-one. You need to adopt strong and effective body language or you will not believe in yourself and the group will not believe in you.

So first, be aware of the body language of leadership. Good leaders seem confident; they use the nonverbal signs of self-assurance such as a 'head up' posture, directive gestures and sure movements. They look directly at other people rather than using the 'down and away' glance of a nervous follower. They do not necessarily shout – in fact if they do they often lose authority rather than gain it – but when they speak, other people listen.

Above and beyond these cues, which simply signal that you are a leader, you then have to involve the people you are with in what you are doing. When you explain things, you need to look round at everyone, making eye contact to draw them all in. Your gestures need to be 'inclusive' – open and towards your body – rather than 'exclusive' – closed and away from your body. And you need to spot anyone whose body language indicates that she (or he) does not feel part of the group, and make a special effort to invite her in, with a questioning look and a smile of welcome.

It can be crucial to control who is speaking and who isn't. If you are using your nonverbal skills correctly, then you will notice who wants to talk because she will raise a finger, lean forward slightly or take an inbreath, in preparation to speak. You will then indicate that you have registered that person by a glance and a nod, and hand over to her when there is a relevant pause. On the other hand, if someone tries to butt in, your direct glance should give that person the message that she should wait her turn.

It is also vital to be able to spot opposition – and cope with it well. You may notice someone with folded arms, an irritated expression or a loud, sharp tone of voice and, if so, you may want to allow that person to express her view. But do not be afraid, as leader, to overrule her, as long as you do it confidently. Studies have shown that most leadership disputes are settled in favour not of the person who argues most convincingly, but in favour of the one who states her case with the most confident body language.

Lastly, you will need to know when the group is really 'behind' you – that is, the point at which you know you have succeeded as a leader. If you notice people looking down, turning slightly away from you or fidgeting noticeably, then you probably have not got full support. If you receive direct eye contact and noticeable nods of agreement, then relax. They are on your side.

How Does My Body Take Time Out When It Needs It?

Like any machine, your body cannot run nonstop. If you have a computer you will know that you regularly have to stop using it so that it can briefly save and process the information you have input. In the same way, brains need time to integrate what they have experienced.

In order to do this, as you work and play you spontaneously take regular 'time out' breaks to process what you are experiencing. If you catch yourself thinking through a problem by looking off into the distance or defocusing, then you are probably taking one of these breaks, even if only for a few seconds.,

But you also need longer breaks. You need more extended time away from stimulation and input. The ultimate break, of course, is sleep, when you take such a noticeable pause that your body shuts out everything, with closed eyes, 'deaf ears', and hardly any movement at all. But when you are not weary enough for sleep you may still need time without stimulation – when you are emotionally stressed, when you need to solve a problem, when you want to think things through. As the most physically arousing thing that a human being can see or hear is another human being, then this means time alone.

Your body's first line of defence when you feel like this is to try to reduce the stimulation naturally, by its own efforts. You may turn or look away, as you may feel unable to maintain eye contact without feeling bad, as if it is just not appropriate for you to be looking at other people. You may find that your normal range of hearing is lessened, as if it just is not appropriate for you to be listening to other people.

If these natural efforts do not work on their own, then your body may signal to you that more dramatic action is needed. It may make you actually feel uncomfortable until you take time out. You may feel tension in your back or jaw, a headache behind your eyes, or a feeling of nausea in your stomach.

And though you may not be aware of it, this discomfort eventually reveals itself on the outside. Your body language tells other people to go away. First, you signal that you are withdrawing from interaction. You become very still, you reduce all gestures, you 'blank out' your facial expression, lower your eyelids, make your voice flat and monotonous. The other person – not getting the lively response he (or she) needs in order to feel appreciated – instinctively cuts down on the interaction, leaving longer pauses between sentences, looking away from you more, eventually falling silent.

Then, if this does not work – because you are surrounded by people, perhaps in the office, on the train, at home – you start to signal more strongly. You develop angular movements, a frown, a jutting mouth; you may shake your head just slightly in a 'no' signal, speak in a sharp, aggressive tone of voice, use abrupt gestures. Without realizing it your body actually signals hostility, in a subconscious effort to force other people to go away.

Pay attention to all these signals. They are your body's way of letting you know that you are on overload. Next time you feel them, retreat to a quiet room with a good book or your favourite video. Staying on good terms with other people may well depend on being prepared to take some time out for yourself.

Can Body Language Help Me to Be More Creative?

You want to be creative – but you are stuck. What is happening? Your mind, instead of first accepting every thought that it has and then choosing the best from a large range, is saying 'no' to every idea. In the end nothing seems right and nothing seems to work.

There are many mental approaches to removing such creative blocks, and many of these approaches are useful. But because your mind is so influenced by your body – and because there are definite body language patterns both to being creative and to being 'blocked' – you can also try experimenting with your nonverbal approach and see if that helps.

People in a creative mood, for example, often display very particular body language patterns. They move easily, their gestures are often 'big' and 'wide', their eye movements sweeping and broad as if to see lots of things. They will take up space as they move, look and gesticulate this way and that. Their expressions are happy and content, in the excitement of being creative.

On the other hand, people who are feeling blocked creatively often display body language patterns that are very different. They sit rigidly, hardly moving, perhaps focused on one point ahead of them, perhaps looking down at the problem they are trying to solve.

When they move they do so hesitantly, perhaps beginning to make gestures, then stopping, shaking their heads and falling still and silent again. Their facial expressions are stressed and unhappy, because every thought they have seems wrong.

The key to changing your uncreative body language to a more creative one is to experiment with all the nonverbal aspects of what you are doing, to find one that allows your body language to become more free and less controlled. Try first of all to alter your environment. Change rooms, find a bigger space, go outside to work. Play music – or stop playing music. Change chairs, to a softer, harder, higher or lower one. Find a bigger table to work on, use larger paper, use different coloured pens.

Alter your posture: lie down, sit up, walk about. Try an uncommon position, such as sitting with your legs crossed; this will distract you from your usual way of thinking by changing your usual way of moving. Use bigger gestures, spreading yourself out across your workspace.

Rather than focusing desperately on the problem in hand, literally look around. Stare out of the window, stare at the ceiling, try going to a higher spot where you can see further. Get a different view of things.

Sooner or later, if you keep experimenting you will find a way of working that succeeds. By freeing up your body you will learn to free up your mind as well.

What Is Stress – and What Can I Do About It?

Stress is increasingly common nowadays. It happens when an inappropriate number of demands are put on your body, without your being able to stop them. So on a physical level, experimental subjects who had to work hard in 38°C (100°F) heat became tense and anti-social. On a more emotional level, subjects asked to cope with unrealistic work deadlines week after week start to suffer the same symptoms.

Interestingly, it can be as stressful to have too little to do as to have too much, because somehow your body gets as frustrated by being under-used as it does by being overstretched.

What happens when you are stressed? When demands are put on your body, chemicals are released into the bloodstream. That is appropriate – once in a while. But if it happens too often, then these chemicals are released into the body at damaging levels, overstimulating all your vital organs and causing all kinds of problems. You may sleep much more or much less, eat much more or much less, gain or lose weight. You may feel constantly irritable, anxious or sad. Your immune system will be worn down by the constant demands on your body – so you may get more colds, more allergies, more skin problems – or worse.

To handle stress, mount a two-pronged attack: long-term coping strategies and emergency measures. Long term, you first have to put a stop to the demands being made on you. If you are in a turbulent relationship, perhaps go to a marriage guidance counsellor. If your job is boring, negotiate for different work conditions.

Then, to help your body cope with day-to-day problems, you should support it physically. A diet low in fat, salt and sugar but high in refined carbohydrates will build health. Less than 28 (for women 21) units of alcohol a week will make sure that your vital organs are not stressed by processing too much. Regular exercise will burn off the chemicals released when you get tense. And regular breaks from work or upsetting family situations will give your body a chance to recuperate.

Also, develop emergency measures to help you cope at the moment stress hits. As you become aware of your stomach churning and your tension rising, take a deep breath. Then let it out gradually, relaxing as you do, to a count of one through ten. Repeat this several times, until you feel yourself beginning to unwind. Make this simple relaxation routine part of your everyday existence; it will make you happier, increase your effectiveness – and help you live longer!

How Can I Build My Self-confidence?

In body language terms, confidence is the physiological proof that you feel able to do what you are about to do. Lack of confidence, on the other hand, is the opposite; it is your body's way of signalling that you are not able to go ahead – and that you really shouldn't be trying to.

Your body signals confidence not only to other people but also to yourself. The signs of lack of confidence are very similar to those of uncertainty and fear – because you are unsure of your capability, and nervous about that. Your gestures will be jerky and uncoordinated; you will show a lack of balance in the way you sit or stand; you will shift position uneasily; you will hesitate or stammer; your stomach may churn and your mouth may go dry.

Recent work in the U.S. in the field of sports psychology suggests that it is possible to teach athletes to be more effective by having them adopt the body language of confidence. And there is no reason to suppose that most things you attempt will not benefit from this approach. This will not work if you simply cannot do what you are trying to do; but if you are capable, and are simply held back by lack of self-belief, then using confident body language may give you the extra physiological boost you need.

To try this, first prepare. Think back to a time when you really were confident, perhaps during your best performance to date. Make sure that your body is firmly balanced, bending your knees

slightly if you are standing, placing yourself squarely on the chair if seated. Keep your spine straight and avoid any side-to-side wobbles. Let go of any signs of tension in your body: drop your shoulders; raise your head and hold it square and facing forward; breathe deeply; smile just slightly, which will also relax you. Check, once again, that your body is centrally balanced and as symmetrical as it can be without tension.

As you do, recall clearly that time you were confident. Take a moment to let the memory really build your confident posture. Use all your body language knowledge and skills to fill your body with enthusiasm and self-belief.

Then, go for it!

2 ♥ Success at Work

How Can Body Language Help Me Succeed at Work?

A lot of research into body language has been funded by – and so focused on – the business world. Therefore there is already a huge body of knowledge within the field of nonverbal communication about the strategies for career success.

Whatever your field – whether you are a skilled worker, an office worker, a manager or a creative wizard – body language can help. First, it shows you what to look for in order to understand your own workplace and your own particular work situation. It helps you analyse what is really going on under the surface, the hidden rules that you need to follow in order to succeed with your colleagues, your employees, your managers, your boss.

Based on these rules, body language then gives you the strategies you need to be able to play the system. It helps you present yourself in a way that will impress – in what you do, what you say, how you act, how you interact. And, as it is sometimes difficult to tell when you are impressing and when not, body language helps further by helping you to read the nonverbal judgements on your performance given by colleagues, customers and clients.

Finally, you will recognize that in business, whether deliberately or through oversight, honesty is not always the only policy. Clients can be unaware of what you need to know; opponents can bend the truth. Body language can help by allowing you to spot what they will not tell you.

In short, body language can allow you to read the secret code behind the words. And that will always give you the edge in your career.

What Does My Workplace Say About the Company I Work for?

Like it or not, your workplace reflects your employers. They will choose the building itself, organize the layout of the workspace, order the furniture and fittings – all to indicate what is important to them and what they want to be important to you.

Is wealth the main aim? There is an accountancy firm in the City of London where the custom-built building is like a fortress. It even has a mock-portcullis and a little gatehouse where you need to check in before visiting. The foyer is huge, lined with marble, and has a picture on the wall that obviously cost more than the average mortgage. This is a firm where money matters, where customers want to be shown that there is real wealth and where the nonverbal signals the firm gives are aimed to reassure and to inspire confidence.

If it is hierarchy that is most vital in your company, watch for the status icons. Directors will have desirable office locations on higher floors, with more windows, more space and more secretaries. They have all the trappings of kingship, such as throne-like swivel chairs with high backs, or a huge, altar-like desk with a reflective surface that will seem to increase the size of the owner's presence. And of course, any company where the managers back-bite about which level of car they are allowed to have is making a nonverbal statement that it is a hierarchical organization.

What if group co-operation is the most important aim? A people business, such as advertising or the media, may use open-plan offices to reinforce co-operative working. There will be perhaps a hundred same-size desks per office, designed to reinforce the view that everyone is equal and can both see and hear each other equally. At the side of this arena there will be lots of dedicated meeting spaces with round tables so that everyone can see each other. There will be a telephone on every desk, and even if the bosses have their own offices they will be glass-walled and will have doors that are jammed permanently open.

Which are more important, the 'customers' or the staff? Consider a supermarket or shop, where the majority of the work area is devoted to the 'punters' and the brightly lit shelves, wide aisles and sparkling customer toilets contrast with the glimpse of tatty shelving or torn-down posters you may get when a 'staff only' door swings open. On the other hand, is yours the kind of company which rarely sees the client, where there is not a single seat to sit on at reception, and an outsider has to shift uneasily from one foot to another until the employee he has come to see wedges another chair beside the desk so that the visitor can sit down?

Whichever general style your workplace follows, you probably cannot change it. But what you can do, not only out of interest but also with the aim of getting ahead, is to use your analysis of that general style to understand more about the company that employs you – and about the values it stands for.

How Can I Customize My Workspace to Meet My Needs?

Does your workspace actually help you work? Is the space the right size? Too little can feel cramped and constricting and can make you feel uncomfortable and distracted. Too much space to work in, as when you are in an open-plan office, may make you feel insecure. If you cannot erect screens, then perhaps you can build your own 'sanity protectors' with stacked files, books or equipment.

Is the furniture right? Whatever kind of work surface you have, you should be able to reach things easily and without strain. Adjust your chair height and buy a footrest if necessary, so that your back is supported and you can move freely. But do not have too comfy a chair, otherwise your body will unwind too much and you will never feel alert at work. And use your work-space to assist what you do: perhaps angling the chairs towards each other if meetings are a large part of your work, turning your desk firmly towards a blank wall if your job demands mostly head-down concentration.

Is yours a noisy environment? Complete silence can be unnerv-ing, but too much noise affects performance because, in a very real sense, you cannot hear yourself think. So unless you are in a job that uses only your physical and not your mental talents (in which case turn up the canned music or take a Walkman to work), reduce the volume – using earplugs if necessary.

Work lighting needs to be bright enough to keep you awake. Slightly dimmed lighting makes you more likely to talk, but less inclined to do physical work or to concentrate. Very dim lighting with a single bright spot shining directly on your desk will con-versely make you less likely to talk but better able to concentrate on the job in hand – a system used in one London translation bureau which presumably wants to encourage its staff to focus on the work they are doing, but not to talk among themselves!

Think about warmth. Most companies nowadays know the health and safety regulation that, once the temperature drops below 16°C (61°F), workers cannot be expected to work produc-tively and must be sent home. Fewer firms know that if the tem-perature goes too high this creates irritation in a workforce, and that a regular temperature dampens spirits. So open the window (if there is one!) if the room gets too hot, and try to take regular breaks in the open air.

Finally, you may want to meet other, less purely professional needs. You may want to keep plants in the office, install a coffee machine on the desk, have your six-year old's latest drawing pinned up on the wall. It is motivating to imprint your personality on your work environment – though, before you do, check that it does not clash with the company culture. One British advertising agency actually instructs its cleaners to bin any personal belong-ings found on employees' desks at night! So observe your office culture carefully and personalize just the amount that is likely to help you make the right impression.

Are There Any Hard-and-fast Guidelines About How I Should Look at Work?

Here is a sobering thought: A survey of 300 top personnel directors said that they judged a potential employee, or someone they were thinking of promoting, mainly on the basis of her (or his) appearance. Performance counted, but the bottom line was that if a person did not look right, then she did not get ahead.

So how should you look? The rulebooks and style guides make it all seem very simple: you need to dress to look attractive and well groomed, you need to dress formally and smartly.

But however many style guides you read, you can still go wrong. For 'looking right' varies from company to company, even from department to department. And this is true whether or not a 'uniform' is part of your job – as it is if you are in the armed forces or medicine. It is true whether or not there are formal dress codes laid down – as there are on the shop floor. Above and beyond these formal codes, every group of people will have developed its own informal style rules. You may not be aware of it, particularly if you are new, but this secret dress code will be there.

This code will partly depend on the nature of your business. Media jobs often encourage you to dress fashionably and brightly, while money jobs prefer conservative dress in dark colours. The code will also depend on your status within a business: the office junior can often wear jeans, the directors cannot. The code will shift with your gender: women are usually allowed to wear more fashionable and colourful clothes than are men. It may even vary according to your department: perhaps the sales force wears suits while the computer team wears chinos.

In fact, this code may actually totally contradict the style guide rules. Wear safe business garb in a creative environment and you may seem boring and without potential. Get your hair coloured, however subtly, for your job in a traditional provincial solicitors' firm and you may be labelled a bimbo (male or female).

The fact is that you have to make any dress decision according to what you personally see around you in the work situation you are in. So check out not what you *think* should happen, but what *actually* happens, in regard to: suit or not; skirt or trousers; dark colours, primaries or pastels; formal or casual; tie pattern, shape and colour; fashion style; jewellery; hair cut; makeup.

Check out too how the rules change in different situations – if you are working out of the office; if you are seeing a client; if you are on site. Check out how the style subtly shifts as one head of department succeeds another who has a totally different style approach. And keep checking. The long painted nails that were acceptable last year may well be seen as tacky this year. The button-down shirt that was the height of fashion when you started in the job may be a black mark on your appraisal by the time you are through your probationary period.

How Can My Body Language Help Me Fit in at Work?

If you are working with other people, then of course you have to be friendly to them. And so you will probably want to use the kind of body language that will make them feel good about you and vice versa.

Psychologists have identified patterns of body language that achieve this, called 'immediacy' patterns. Immediacy body language includes facing people directly, looking at them, leaning towards them as they speak, having a friendly expression, smiling. You probably know and use all these signals regularly in your social life.

But beware using them inappropriately at work. At work, you need to get the job done and not confuse the issue with too much friendly feeling. So tone down your immediacy with more formal body language. Do not approach too close. Do not smile, giggle or laugh overmuch. And tone down any expression of negative emotion, such as tears or tantrums, that might draw any of your colleagues into a more personal relationship with you.

That said, of course the rules do vary. Some companies are comfortable with very immediate body language, others prefer a very formal style. Some departments, such as creative ones, tend to be more immediate in their nonverbal approach than others. Some people – such as clients and managers – will by their presence shift the body language temporarily; the noise level will spontaneously go down and employees will be less likely to visit each other's desks, drop things or lean back in their chairs.

And some specific situations call for different body language approaches. After a company catastrophe, such as redundancies or a big drop in sales, then immediacy will rise – you may well move close to each other, touch to comfort or show strong emotion, at least until the crisis is over. At the other end of the scale, in a promotion interview you will almost certainly be more formal than you otherwise would be, even towards colleagues with whom you are normally quite friendly. Once the interview is over and your promotion has been announced, on the other hand, you may celebrate by hugging and kissing!

What Is the Pecking Order at Work, and Why Should I Worry About It?

In any group of birds, some get to peck the corn first, others later. A group of birds will arrange themselves in an informal but strict status hierarchy – the 'pecking order'. And so will any group of humans.

If the group is a work team or department, then very often the formal boss or manager is at the top of the pecking order – if not, then he (or she) will find it hard to keep control and command. But even if everyone in a group is equal in terms of salary and status, its members will take up a personal pecking order – which may have nothing to do with work values. Being top may be about being married, being fashionable, having children or being the one who throws parties, just as much as about being good at the job, working hard or being next in line for promotion.

Pecking order is not something you talk about. It may not even be something most people are conscious of. But everyone in a particular group will unconsciously reflect the pecking order by his or her body language. So, for example, there will be a totally unspoken order of who takes precedence in meetings. Who pops into whose office without knocking, who takes space in filing cabinets without permission or who can fill the corner of the car park with his camper van without anyone else complaining.

Often, pecking order is about who does things and who has things done for him. And this is one reason why, in order to make managers seem higher in the pecking order, they often have assistants to help them. The lower in the pecking order you are, the more you will be expected to make the tea, go out for sandwiches, fetch and carry. But it does work both ways – if you are high in the pecking order, you may be expected to play 'lord (or lady) bountiful' – lending your possessions or inviting others to dinner. It is expected, for example, for a boss to buy a 'round' in a situation where the office junior just would not – unless it were your birthday, an occasion which immediately raises you in the pecking order, just for the day!

What if someone steps outside his pecking order? Then, as if by magic the whole group will unconsciously close ranks against the upstart. If you interrupt someone above you in the pecking order, then he will just talk over you and the group will stare you down. If you walk without knocking into the office of someone above you in the pecking order, you will receive a frosty stare, if not an actual reprimand. So be aware of what the pecking order is in your company – and tread carefully. It could make the difference between being accepted and being ostracized!

How Can Body Language Help Me Steer Clear of 'Office Politics'?

Most office politics boils down to 'who sides with whom?' To avoid getting caught up in the conflict, first spot the groups that are siding with each other.

Every group will nonverbally signal its identity. Members of one group may display what are called 'tie' signs, signals that they identify with each other. They may wear the same kind of suit. They may encourage each other to have their hair styled the same way. They will all go off for a smoke together. They will mark out little areas as their 'territory', pushing desks together, gathering at the same table in the canteen, perhaps even placing actual barriers, such as a filing cabinet or a plant, at the entrance to their area of the workspace.

This group identity may differ from that of another group in the same office. Look for slightly different styles of dress, one group wearing jeans while the other wears leggings. Look for different activities; one group going down to the pub while the other brings in sandwiches. Already, you have the foundations of opposition.

But do you have hostility? In work situations, people often try to hide what they really feel, so the signals may be subtle. Look for an absence of normal social contact: do the members of one group hang back from visiting the desks of the other? When they do, do they scarcely smile, rarely stop and chat, keep their remarks short and brusque? Do they lean backwards, keep a blank expression, shake their heads fractionally when listening to the others talk? You may notice 'leakages' of hostility – unconscious, fleeting facial expressions of anger or frustration coming through the normally bland and friendly working mask.

Can you steer clear of all that? It can be difficult, because you may well naturally side with one group rather than the others – and your body language may reveal this whether you want it to or not. But if tension in your work situation is such that you need to tread a determinedly neutral path, then you have to behave towards all sides in a way that shows equal nonverbal approval. So balance out any 'tie' signs that bind you with any particular side; wear jeans one day and leggings the next. Avoid any activities that seem to demonstrate loyalty; if one group invites you to the wine bar, then be sure to go to the gym next day with another. Chat with members of all groups. When you pass on the corridor, give everyone the same friendly smile.

You could almost do a mental check at the end of each day: Have you spent as much time, with as many members, of each of the opposing groups? If not, then tomorrow redress the balance.

How Can I Stand Up to the Office Bully?

Every company has an office bully, even if the other members of staff keep her (or him) under control. The bully is not likely to be a high-status person; more likely she (or he) is someone who is unsure of herself, but hides that with bluster. Look perhaps for a person whose slumped shoulders and downturned mouth tell you that she feels negative about life and will let that frustration out on others. Or look for someone whose slight swagger and sharp, aggressive tone of voice tell you that she would like to be leader of the pack – but not having the charisma of a natural leader, has settled instead for trying to dominate anyone who will let her do so.

For a bully is always someone who actually lacks self-esteem. Bullying boosts the bully's confidence by destroying someone else's. So whereas in a normal conflict at work you can usually resolve things by talking them through, with a bully this is not possible. Her only aim is simply to hurt – by calling names, by spoiling your work, sometimes by actual violence. And because of this, a bully will always choose to pick on people who look as if they will allow themselves to be hurt, will give up easily, will not fight back. The bottom line is that if your body language signals all these things, then you stand more of a chance of being bullied. If your body language instead signals self-confidence, then the bully may well leave you alone.

Begin by being aware of the particular set of body language signs that, in apes as well as humans, indicates 'loser'. Then make sure you are not showing any of these signs. Straighten your shoulders rather than hunching them. Look directly forward rather than away. Put aside nervous mannerisms, like chewing your hair, playing with your tie, scratching your head, smiling apologetically. Start mixing with colleagues who are also confident; a bully goes for loners, and will rarely tackle someone if he or she is surrounded by friends.

If the bully does approach you, stay calm. Do your best to ignore what is happening, taking a deep breath to remove tension, looking directly at the bully and, if you possibly can, simply acting as if she is a fool. The alternative is to go onto the attack: pull yourself up to full height, head up, look at the bully almost down your nose and keep your face serious – a smile can be a sign of appeasement as well as of amusement. In a loud, clear, angry voice tell her to go away. Then walk off.

If you are genuine and can really act as if the whole thing does not threaten you, then the bully will start to believe that you are not an easy victim. In the end she will look elsewhere, lose interest and forget you even exist.

What Is the Secret Body Language of Sex at Work?

Lots of people fall in love at work. But because work is supposed to be about business rather than intimacy, often lovers have to hide their relationship – particularly if, as sometimes happens, one partner or both are already committed elsewhere! So sex at work is often secret. How can you spot it?

If you are with someone you suspect of being lovesick, watch him (or her) as the possible object of affection appears. Unconsciously, he will actually look more attractive; his muscle tone will spontaneously increase, his lips will become slightly fuller – even the bags under his eyes may go down! He will automatically begin to show off his best points – turn his head to show a 'best side', pull in his stomach, sit up straight to show off broad shoulders (or full female breasts if the unrequited lover is female). He may start 'preening', improving his appearance by adjusting his collar, smoothing back his hair, licking his lips – (or as one group of young men were seen to do when a certain female manager entered the room, all straightening their ties in unison!).

As time goes by, you may then watch fascinated as both parties in the potential love relationship start to recognize their mutual attraction and to signal it to each other. Even if they think they are hiding what is happening, there will be subtle signs typical of people in love (or in lust). They will hold eye contact, looking more than usual and with less blinking than normal. They will use a slightly different tone of voice (low and husky) with each other than with any other colleagues. They may reveal a tendency to block off other people from intruding on their developing relationship by turning their backs to the room when they are together, or failing to see or hear attempts to interrupt their conversation.

Suddenly, a few days later, all these signals seem to stop. The lovers ignore each other on the corridor, exchange only polite greetings in the lift. Their expressions are completely blank, or even slightly hostile. They may begin to disagree with each other in a way they never did before. What is happening?

Possibly they have tried to create a relationship and it has failed. Their body language reflects the fact that they feel angry with each other and are trying to erase the memory. But it could be the total opposite: their relationship may have gone beyond flirting and they do not want anyone else to spot just how far it has gone.

So check the couple's unconscious body language signals. Are they still 'pointing' to each other with their bodies – elbows, feet, hand gestures all indicating the other person? Have they begun to 'match' each other, taking up the same body positions, using the same gestures at the same time, picking up the same turns of phrase?

If they are displaying these real signs of intimacy, then ignore the seeming hostility. It is a smoke screen to put observant people like you off the scent!

How Does the Way I Use My Time Affect How My Colleagues See Me?

Your use of time makes a powerful nonverbal statement in your work situation every day about how efficient you are, how committed you are and how important you think you are.

The most basic statement you make is whether you are on time or not. Most companies see latecomers as also being inefficient and bad at their job, whether or not they are – and even if you are operating a flexitime system, there will be a cut-off time such as eleven o'clock, after which you will be judged as late even if you worked until midnight the day before.

But strangely, being early at work can also make a negative statement. Coming in to work early may indicate that you cannot handle your responsibilities within the normal 9-to–5 day. Arriving more than a quarter of an hour early for a meeting can indicate that you haven't got anything else important to do – and therefore that you are not doing an important job. And getting through a job too quickly and handing it in ahead of schedule can make people feel you have not done it well enough.

If you are paid by the hour and do overtime, the main statement this makes is that you need the money. If you are on salary, however, working after hours gets you noticed. Studies have shown that those who stay late in the evening tend to be seen as more central to the company, get consulted more about decisions, and are more likely to get promotion. On the other hand, in some companies working late is the norm, not the exception. Then if you do *not* stay late you are seen as slacking, and will get passed over for promotion even if, on paper, you are doing your statutory 40 hours and getting all the required work done on time.

The higher up you are in a company, the more you can misuse the time of others. At the bottom of the ladder your time is not your own, but your boss's. At the very top other people's time is at your disposal. You can extend meetings to suit you, change the timing of events, ask others to work late, tell them to come in early. You can keep them waiting in an outer office for hours – or days. You can be unavailable. The nonverbal message in the work situation is that the more important you are, the more valuable is your time compared to that of others.

How Can I Be More Effective on the Telephone?

Body language is not just about what you see, but also about what you hear. The volume of a voice, its speed, tone, rhythm, pitch, accent and stress will all give you information about the person on the other end of the line. And your voice will affect your caller, making her (or him) more likely to co-operate with you – or not.

Use body language initially to make sure that you sound positive on the phone. If you are slumped in a chair with your head down, or if you are tense while phoning, you will sound tired; if your throat is restricted, research has shown that you may also sound insincere. On the other hand, a trick used by telesales people is to sit up and smile; your more cheerful physical state will transmit itself through your voice. Of course you may not be able to stand up during every phone call, but you can always sit up straight, and yawn beforehand to relax your jaw muscles.

Next, as you start the call and exchange greetings, listen carefully to the voice of the person on the other end of the phone. This allows you to pick up, from her tone of voice, just what sort of person she is and what kind of mood she is in. Is this an impatient customer, with a rushed, high tone of voice; a calm client with a slow, even speed? What does the stress she puts on different words tell you about what is important to her in what you are discussing?

Notice particularly if the caller's voice changes. For often, way before someone's words reveal that her mood or attitude has altered, her voice will reveal this. A caller whose voice suddenly rises may be starting to get irritated. A caller whose voice suddenly drops, or who starts to hesitate between words, is perhaps becoming unsure. If you spot this, you can alter your approach to suit.

Really successful telephone talkers go one step further: They not only analyse the person they are talking to from her voice cues, they also spontaneously 'match' the other person's voice. You may have found yourself doing this with someone who has a strong regional accent – and then felt embarrassed at appearing to be mimicking her. In fact, this kind of spontaneous copying is barely noticeable to the listener and, as imitation is the sincerest form of flattery, can actually be quite reassuring. So although it is unwise to do so deliberately, if you find yourself picking up on your caller's voice patterns, then you may well find that things go better.

Be aware of when the other person wants to end the call. Her speed may increase as if to hurry things up – or alternatively you may notice longer and longer silences between words. On the other hand, you may sense from the caller's tone of voice and a slight intake of breath down the line, that she has something more to say; stay on the line and give her the chance to do that.

Finally, make sure that the last words you speak sound cheerful, leaving the caller with a clearly positive impression of you.

How Can I Best Meet My Clients' Needs?

Different clients want different things, above and beyond a good business deal. And if you do not meet their needs nonverbally, you may find yourself failing to satisfy without really knowing why.

Some clients like to be in charge. If you work in a service industry, your client may be used to having his demands met. He is the kind of person who has developed his own, controlling body language style to achieve this, looking serious and dominant, making leadership gestures that direct you round your own workspace, and using a clear voice that is completely at home with giving orders.

If what is important is keeping this client happy, then place him at the head of the table, in a high-backed chair; position yourself to one side. Keep standing until he sits, nod a good deal when he is speaking, let him feel in control because of your deferential body language.

But if what is important is to meet this client on equal terms – whether or not this destroys the deal – then shift the balance to a more equal one by sitting adjacent at a square meeting table; using chairs of equal-backed height; standing just as tall as he does; taking on a 'plus' expression (head erect, direct gaze and a neutral rather than placatory look on your face); and matching his dominant tone of voice with a firm, clear one of your own.

A second kind of client is one who needs to know that you are the expert. You are likely to be in a specialist industry, or selling a specialist product, and the client needs to rely on your knowledge. He may show his lack of certainty by a slightly nervous manner – or by a belligerence that is underpinned by nervousness. Underneath, he simply wants to be given the answers.

If you do have the knowledge and can provide a good service, then make sure that your body language reassures. Sit at the head of the table as if in charge, placing the client to one side. Stand to make your presentation, and use confident body language, your gaze direct, your gestures assured, your tone of voice firm and steady in a way that stresses your knowledge and capability. Use diagrams and charts to emphasize that you know what you are doing well enough that you can put it down in black and white.

What about the client to whom personal contact is vital? If you are both in the people business, or in a co-operative profession rather than a competitive one, your client needs to feel good about you in order to do business with you. He will tend to call you by your first name, to ask about your personal life. He will use friendly body language, with smiles, easy gestures, meeting and parting hugs.

If you return your client's feeling for personal contact as the basis for professional dealings, then show this in your body language. Come down to the foyer to meet him and escort him personally to your office. Seat yourselves side by side or angled across a 'meeting sofa', then serve coffee, as you would to a friend. Notice yourself 'matching' or paralleling the way the client sits or moves – a sign that the two of you understand each other enough to copy one another spontaneously.

In short, however good the service you are offering, you also need to convince nonverbally. If you do, the client will be satisfied – and you will get repeat business.

Can I Use Body Language Techniques to Achieve a Good Relationship with a Retail Customer?

Yes, you can. Use these techniques first to spot just the right moment to approach. Do not rush up to store customers who are 'just looking', as this can make them feel pressured. Instead, keep an eye on the customer who pauses at a particular item, reaches out and touches it, then perhaps picks it up so as to see it better. Just after this, there will be a precise moment when she (or he) looks around, eyebrows raised in an 'appeal look'. That is when she will welcome help, and that is when you can best start selling.

Begin by making contact. Look at the customer as you approach. Smile as you greet her – a universal signal of friendliness and reassurance. Then take up a position at an angle from her – directly opposite can seem too confrontational and creates a situation where you are seen as challenging the customer to buy.

Once having made contact, the tradition is to offer sales 'talk' – but it actually works better to use sales 'show', presenting your range to a customer and then reading her body language to judge what suits. As you do, develop the good relationship by making the customer the centre of your attention. Keep your focus on her, body, head and eyes all angled in her direction; turning away, looking away, speaking to someone else or fidgeting all give the non-verbal message that the customer and her purchase do not matter. Make your tone of voice warm, with interest and encouragement showing through. Do not smile too much once the first contact is made, as this can seem over-familiar, but keep a friendly expression – and an interested tilt of the head if that comes naturally to you.

If you can, give a brief touch. Place a hand on her arm while the customer is trying on a watch, a guiding hand to usher her into a changing room. Touching is one way to build good feeling, and studies have shown that sales assistants who touch a customer are three times more likely to achieve a sale. Timing is crucial, though; touch a person too soon and she will feel threatened, leave it too late and you will lose the effect.

Also be aware of the point where a customer starts to retreat. She may back off from the purchase and from her 'relationship' with you, perhaps because she is starting to get embarrassed for taking so long. She may start using 'blocking' body language, turning to one side, losing eye contact, placing her arms across her body, hugging a briefcase or bag for comfort. It can be tempting at this point to 'up the ante', but this will only make the customer feel pressured. Instead, wait with your attention still firmly on the customer, which may provide the nonverbal 'space' for her to get involved once again.

What if she doesn't? If she gives 'ready to go' signals, such as stepping back from the counter or looking towards the exit, then help her to leave – she will be far more likely to come back. Apologize for not having what she needs, and say goodbye with a smile that promises a welcome when she returns.

How Can I Really Tell When I Have Closed a Sale?

Whether your 'sale' is on the retail floor or in the boardroom, then it is useful to be able to tell whether you have closed it or not.

A customer or client thinking things through will probably fall silent for a few moments. If his (or her) eyes engage yours for a few seconds with a slight encouraging smile, then he is probably looking for input from you; if you tilt your head in enquiry, he may ask you the question he wants answered. If he turns and looks away from you, however, then he wants to consider the options alone.

A person still making his mind up also displays a number of 'indecision' signals. These usually involve some kind of imbalance, almost as if the person's body is 'weighing the options'. So you may notice a shake of the head from one side to the other, a wiggle of the shoulders, or a shift of weight from one foot to the other. One explanation of this is that the spinal cord, running down the centre of the body, carries signals to all parts – and if the signals are contradictory or uncertain, then this results in movement on first one side of the body, then the other. If you notice such imbalanced signals while a client is thinking, then do not interrupt.

When the thinking is done, and the client gives his answer, keep checking his body language – whether what he says is a 'yes' or a 'no'. For sometimes what the client says may not be what he means.

A client who says and means 'no' will usually shake his head firmly as he utters the refusal. Then he will be less likely to look you in the eye, almost as if afraid of seeing any bad reaction you may have. He will often try to pull away and leave quite quickly, as if wary that you will now pressure him. He will move to the edge of his chair immediately and start making gestures towards the exit; his handshake will be light and hasty.

An unsure as opposed to a definite 'no' has a very different non-verbal pattern. The client will keep looking at you as he states the refusal, turned towards you, head on one side. He wants to be convinced, so he wants to keep contact, to see more of you and hear more of what you have to say. It is worth while trying to convert this into a yes.

When you get that yes, look for just how definite it is. Do you still see signs of uncertainty? If so, check out what the client's reservations are. But if you see direct eye contact, an unambiguous nod of agreement, a smile of reassurance and a prolonged and definite final handshake, then celebrate. You have made the sale.

What Are People's Hidden Agendas at Meetings?

Everyone has her (or his) own aims and goals in a meeting – and most people mix and match. If someone has a particular agenda, you may find that her nonverbal behaviour follows a particular pattern.

hello!

hello!

Who arrives on time, eager to start, willing to chat but only to the people who might be useful to her during the meeting? She is the one who will be most keen to get things done, least likely to get distracted. Who arrives slightly early, in company with others that she has already met before the discussion starts? She is likely to consider people important and be wary of any decisions that alienate staff. What about the latecomer? If she is calm and unhurried as she arrives, then the meeting may not be all that important to her. But if she makes an entrance and demands attention as she comes in, then her lateness may be a powerplay; watch out for her attempts to gain control during the meeting.

Where do people naturally sit? If placings are not predetermined, then the person who gravitates to the central point of a long side of a meeting table will be most likely to take everyone into account – though she may also have the most control simply by being best able to see what is happening. 'End sitters' like to get things done, often by directing or sometimes by bullying the team; their second-in-commands often sit just 'round the corner' from them. Opponents often make sure they sit opposite each other, while those who work together are often, quite literally, 'on the same side'.

What do people concentrate on during the meeting? A 'people person' will keep looking and listening at other delegates; you may actually see her head turning, as if during a tennis match, to get as much input from other participants as possible. Someone who utilizes objects as 'props' – opening a folder, waving a piece of paper, slamming down a glass – may well be interested in control; she will focus on objects because things are more manageable than people are. And the delegate who focuses on the agenda and the clock at the expense of everything else will be someone who wants to get things done.

When it comes to leaving the meeting, each delegate will have her or his own style. The 'getting things done' delegate checks in briefly with the people she needs to do business with, waves a general goodbye to others, and leaves quickly to be on time for her next meeting. Someone who wants to be in control of the situation will say goodbye only to the higher-status people, with a light touch or handshake; research suggests that touching people in a power situation makes them more manageable. The 'people person' too will touch, but in a sociable way – an arm touch, a friendly hug or (for women) a kiss on the cheek. This delegate will make sure to say goodbye to everyone in the room and will exit with a friendly smile.

How Can I Use Body Language to Help Meetings Go Well?

What is said at meetings is only the tip of the iceberg. Underneath lies a whole layer of body language signals that can alert you to delegates' thoughts and feelings. If you are leading a meeting – or are in a position to influence it – then you can act as soon as you read these signals.

Who is really involved, and who is just marking time? A delegate who leans forward with his legs drawn back under him, whose head is alertly tilted and whose eyes open slightly wider in response to a key point is genuinely interested – while one who leans back with his legs stretched out, his head turned away or demonstrating a total lack of eye movement is not really feeling involved or absorbed. You might want to draw that delegate into the discussion by inviting him to speak, and then rewarding his contribution with the natural human 'acknowledgement' signals of a slight smile and the occasional slow nod.

At the other end of the scale, what about someone who wants to contribute? You may notice such signals as direct and fixed eye contact with the chairperson to try and make contact; an irritated expression with lowered brows; a sharp intake of breath as if preparing to speak; or a raised finger or pen – a gesture that survives from having to raise a hand to speak in school! If you do spot these signs, look fixedly at the delegate who is giving them – that will focus other people's attention, and will ensure that the delegate is heard.

Who agrees with whom? Body language often reflects mental approach, and you can often tell which people are on the same side because they may be sitting in the same sort of posture and using the same kind of gestures. If one person moves and another shifts position directly afterwards, then you can be pretty certain that they are broadly in sympathy. If one of them then changes to copy a member of the opposing 'team', then you need to be prepared for a transfer of loyalty!

Outright disagreement is easily spotted: people frown, shake their heads and shout! But watch too for early signs of rising irritation. Glancing away can reveal impatience – literally an unwillingness to see the other person and his point of view. Lowered eyebrows and pursed lips reflect ape 'anger' signs, and can spell trouble. Crossed arms can mean a defensive attitude (though they can also mean a cold room!). In all these cases you may well want to use a calm tone of voice and soothing gestures to compose the meeting – or a sharp firm tone and decisive gestures to bring the delegates to order.

Lastly, as the meeting nears its end, it is worth checking that decisions have really been agreed by everyone in the room. If when you review proposed action people look away or shift in their seats, this shows they are unsure or will not in practice back your plan. Keep the discussion going until, when you summarize the agreements, you see delegates looking at you steadily and giving a slight nod – this means you have their agreement, and their co-operation.

How Can I Recognize a Liar in Business?

Recognizing when business contacts are aware of something 'wrong' in what they are saying is fairly easy; there are clear signals that reveal this. The problem is that in business people can give out such signals for reasons other than that they are lying. They may be telling the truth, but know that what they are saying will be unwelcome. They may be telling the truth, but not really want to be telling it. So read the nonverbal clues you see within the context of the situation you are in. That said, when someone says something that she knows to be 'wrong', a number of things are obvious. First, her body finds it difficult to allow her to speak. She may put her fingers slightly across her mouth, as if to stifle the words. She may use the 'choker' gesture in which the hand goes to the throat, as if to stop herself speaking. Even if she does not do this, her throat muscles may close so that you may hear a slight rise in pitch or vocal tremor. If the words do come out, they may do so in a confused way: the person may stutter, hesitate, mumble, switch words or sentences around, or get halfway through one phrase and then switch to another.

Also, a liar's body, aware of all these give-away signals, may try to mask them. So a person may deliberately 'blank out' her body language: she will turn away slightly, or turn her head to one side; she will stand unusually still; she will use fewer gestures than usual; she will keep her expression fixed. Particularly, she may keep her hands still, and turned inwards – studies suggest that it is easier for people to fib if the palms of their hands are held downwards and out of view. She may try to show that she is unconcerned by direct eye contact and a bright smile, but end up using the 'false smile' which reaches the lips but does not engage the muscles round the eyes.

Underneath all this masking, a liar is nevertheless sending out all kinds of nervous signals because she is afraid of getting spotted. These signs will not easily be seen, and will not appear at all in those parts of the body that are most on show, such as the face. But far away from that 'centre stage', at the periphery of the body, a liar's fingers may be fidgeting, toes twitching, feet tapping as if trying to escape. And the unconscious, uncontrollable signals of stress, from the nervous system, will come to the surface regardless; so a liar may have uneven breathing, a tendency to clear her throat, a sudden change in skin colour, or a dry mouth that causes her to lick her lips more often.

If you do suspect that a colleague is not telling the truth, then often there is simply nothing you can do about it. Sometimes, however, it may be possible to challenge her by using body language which makes it more difficult for her to lie. The more directly and closely a person is challenged by another, the more uncomfortable she will be if she is lying. So move close, face your colleague directly, get eye contact, and take on a serious, unapologetic expression. Then ask your question again. This time, you may hear the truth.

How Can I Defend Myself Against Sexual Harassment?

Whether you are a woman or a man, sexual harassment can be a problem. How can you avoid it?

Your first line of defence could well be to make sure that your appearance simply cannot be misinterpreted. The hard fact is that, particularly in a work context, sexy dress can attract unwelcome attention – and this applies to both sexes. Of course it is beyond argument that whatever you wear and whatever your body language, you have an inalienable right not to be sexually intimidated. Even so, some people interpret certain signals incorrectly, and therefore it is sound practice to leave at home the icons of sexuality, such as black leather, red lipstick, flowing hair, tight trousers or an open shirt, in favour of the icons of professional inaccessibility, such as tailored suits and a neat appearance.

Your second line of defence is awareness. If you can spot sexual harassment the minute it begins, then you have a much better chance of stopping it. So unless you want a relationship with a colleague, be wary of any behaviour that even hints at attraction. Take care if someone watches you constantly, gives you the overlong eye contact typical of a lover, comes within your intimate distance of 45 cm (18 in), or 'accidentally' touches you and then strongly denies that anything happened.

It can be difficult to react disapprovingly because to do so is so socially untypical. You may think that you are imagining what is happening; but even if you are, it is fairer on all concerned to signal immediately that you feel uncomfortable. So indicate your unease at these things as early as possible. Show that you feel invaded; step back out of intimate distance, fold your arms across your body and turn away. Show your disapproval by frowning, and speaking in a clipped and frosty tone of voice. You can nip suggestive behaviour in the bud by revealing your disapproval clearly at the start.

What if the worst happens? Suggestions are made, an accidental touch lingers, a hand is placed where it should not be. This kind of harassment is not about sex but about power, so the most effective reaction is a direct and powerful challenge. React immediately and strongly, with no equivocation. Pull yourself up to your full height, pushing your harasser back, speaking loudly to draw attention to what is happening. Say 'No, don't!'; 'How dare you talk like that to me!', or even 'Does this hand belong to anyone?' If you can both embarrass your harasser and make other people a witness to the embarrassment, then you may not have to make a formal complaint. You will have shown that you are as powerful as your oppressor, and you may never be troubled again.

How Can I Handle a Difficult Boss?

What do you do with a difficult boss, one who gets irritated, angry, nervous or irrational? The problem is that you cannot simply react towards him (or her) in the way you would towards a friend – shouting back at his irritation, calming his nerves with a hug or a drink. For, to some extent, even with the most democratic boss you do need to maintain some remnants of what you might call 'subordinate' body language – respectful and unchallenging. So what can you do?

An aggressive boss, one who responds to pressure by shouting, making hostile gestures or even throwing things, can be very disturbing. He may not actually be angry at you – but he is aiming the emotion in your direction. Faced with your boss's aggression, your body may well quite spontaneously, and understandably, react with panic or with equal anger. So see to your own physiological needs first, breathing deeply in order to lower your heart rate and pulse rate, perhaps even carrying out a quick relaxation drill by tensing your whole body deliberately and then consciously letting your muscles slacken.

Then try not to increase your boss's aggression by confrontational body language. Look down at the desk rather than directly staring into his eyes, turn away slightly rather than taking up an aggressive posture with shoulders squared.

As soon as you can, say quietly but firmly that you are going to find some papers. Do not even look at your boss – for a permission which he may refuse – but simply leave the room and wait a few minutes to allow things to cool down. Then return with a friendly expression, behaving as if nothing has happened.

A boss who gets nervous or even panicky under pressure needs slightly different handling. Here his random gestures, shaky or distracted voice, pacing round the room or nervous habits will tell you that something has happened to put him off balance. What he does not need is for you to get disturbed by this – because then he will have to handle your panic as well as his own. So once again make sure you are imperturbable, perhaps going through the relaxation drill mentioned above.

You do not need to leave the room in this situation; if you do, your boss may feel unsupported. Instead, let your unruffled posture show that you are calm, and simply keep watching as he paces about. Psychologists suggest that giving others your attention, even if no words are spoken, may well actually relax them physiologically, so be prepared to do this for several seconds or even a few minutes. You will be able to tell that your boss is feeling steadier when his movements slow and he looks at you as if seeing you rather than seeing through you. This is the point at which you can start to offer practical help.

How Can I Tell Whether I Am Doing Well in Work or Not?

It can be very difficult to assess what people really think of your work. Sometimes they do not know, sometimes they will not say. Sometimes the only way is to read their nonverbal signals, which are a direct line to their real judgement whether they know it or not.

So what if a manager or colleague approves of what you have done? The obvious signs are an approving smile, a tone of voice that rises with enthusiasm, a brief celebratory touch on your shoulder or arm. But a boss who is not a 'people person' may not feel comfortable doing any of these things, so what should you look for? The most basic approval movement in most cultures of the Western world is a forward nod; however restrained someone is being she (or he) will find it difficult not to give a tiny nod like that when she sees something that feels good to her. Equally, if something is satisfactory many people add a slow outbreath to the nod – not a shudder of frustration but a barely noticeable contented sigh.

You need to be careful, however. All the approval signs mentioned above can be faked by someone who does not dare tell you her real thoughts about your work. Watch particularly for a false smile, which unlike a real one starts and fades just too slowly, tends to get stuck at its widest point and, because it does not use the muscles around the eyes, never seems to touch the person's whole face.

Clear disapproval is fairly easy to spot; you do not need body language skills to know when you are being shouted at! You will probably be able to recognize even mild disapproval – a puckering of the forehead, the lowered eyebrows of irritation, a faster tone of voice, a short sharp outbreath. All these signs reveal irritation and frustration.

But what if someone is not sure what she feels, or dare not be clear about negative feelings? Watch for the most basic disapproval movement in most Western cultures, the shake of the head. It is said to have developed from the movement all humans use as babies to refuse food by turning away from it – and is often accompanied by the closed mouth, pursed lips or slightly protruding tongue that a baby uses when she does not want to be fed!

The most useful response, of course, is to ask your colleague to say more about her reservations. And the most useful accompanying body language is the slightly tilted head and questioning glance that lets you ask a person, in the most unthreatening way, to say more about what she feels. Reassured that you are not going to get angry in return, the hesitant critic may well be persuaded to say how you could improve. You may well end up gaining more approval for being able to handle feedback than disapproval for your original error!

Are There Nonverbal Tactics I Can Use to Get Ahead?

It would be nice to think that sheer talent and expertise gets you promotion. But in fact most people who are promoted fulfil one other key requirement: they act in ways that fulfil their company's unspoken criteria.

So look carefully at all the elements of your body language. You may want to read the sections of this book on dress (*page 45*), workspace (*page 43*), use of time (*page 54*) and person-to-person style (*page 47*). Aim to meet your company's criteria in all these areas, taking your model from the best practice of the level you are already on, but also looking at what happens in the level above you – what is known as 'aspirational' body language.

Are you, for example, still dressing as if you are a junior? Should you be wearing a more expensive suit or more subtle makeup? The higher up the company you go, the more likely it is that you will be expected to dress expensively and stylishly – employees have been kept at their current level for decades because they insisted on wearing nylon shirts!

Does your workspace still look as if you are on a level lower than your own? Is there no computer in sight in a company where the top people get the biggest screens – if so, start throwing temper tantrums until you get one too. On the other hand, if the bosses have clear desks and only the typists use word processors, then you might wonder about keeping your computer firmly switched off, or even putting it back in its box!

Are you still organizing your time as if you were a worker rather than a manager – with most of your day spent doing the job yourself, when the company now wants to see you scheduling meetings to guide and brief other people?

In particular, how are you acting towards those above you in the company? You should not be aping them by using exactly the same nonverbal signals as they do – for that will threaten the hierarchy and people will automatically block your progress. On the other hand, be wary of being too subservient in the hope that it will curry favour. Overpleasant, placating smiles, a syrupy tone of voice and submissive body language may make your boss feel superior to you, but it will also make him see you as someone who is naturally subservient. He will not be able to imagine you being self-directed, taking responsibility, or managing staff. As a result he may find it impossible to conceive of you ever moving up in the firm.

How Might My Body Language Alter When I Get Promotion?

You have been appointed team leader or made manager. Of course this will cause changes in your job. And one of the things that you may notice changing is your body language. If you succeed as a leader, then quite spontaneously you will start putting out different nonverbal signs – the more authoritative signals of 'leadership'.

You may, for example, notice that you are more 'formal' with subordinates – even with people who used to be good friends. In order to manage them, you have to keep your distance somehow, showing colleagues less of what you are really thinking and feeling. So you may tend to control your posture, use more directive gestures, keep a more fixed expression, speak more deliberately and less emotionally.

You will also begin to use body language that shows that you have privileges. In a meeting you will sit more centrally. You will expect to talk first, talk longest, to interrupt subordinates and not to be interrupted by them. If you make a suggestion, you will expect it to be acted on. You will feel better able to move into a subordinate's space, enter without knocking, approach her (or his) desk more closely.

Interestingly, when dealing with superiors your body language may actually become more informal after your promotion, because you are now more their equal. Rather than being nonverbally 'on the alert' as if to do their bidding, you will find yourself sitting in a more relaxed way, smiling and laughing with them more, even touching them to make contact or offer support. They in return will be more relaxed with you, perhaps calling you by your first name, inviting you to the pub or to their house.

Is it possible to become a better manager by deliberately taking on 'leadership' body language? The answer is a definite maybe. If you do, then perhaps you will immediately feel more confident and begin to act that way naturally; confidence underpins all successful leadership body language. This may well work, particularly in a situation where you are managing people who do not already know you. Simply by adopting more formal and more 'privileged' body language you will start acting like a leader, you will encourage them to think of you as a leader, and they will.

But using the body language of a leader may backfire on you. You may find it difficult to maintain, and other people may find it difficult to accept – particularly if they used to be your friends or colleagues. They will react resentfully or mockingly, and you will struggle to keep control. So if you have been promoted to a new position within an old situation, you may have to allow your new, more authoritative body language to grow with the job.

Whichever route you take, if you are successful in your new role then a few months or years down the road you will almost certainly notice a shift in your body language. You will be acting like a boss – and other people will be treating you like one.

How Can I Best Motivate My Staff?

Challenging jobs, increased pay packages, better working conditions – all of these are vital to job motivation. But studies have shown that the way you encourage or reprimand staff is just as big an incentive.

When rewarding staff, whether informally by a quick 'Well done' or formally with a certificate or medal, you will make them feel even better by using positive body language. Go right up to them, smile approvingly, give them just a few moments' complete attention to show that their contribution is important.

If appropriate – and only if appropriate – mark your feelings by actual contact – research done with sports teams reveals that competitors, for example, felt even better if congratulations were accompanied by a shoulder slap or light touch.

Telling staff to do something differently – or again – also needs appropriate body language. All too often, because you feel so frustrated, you can fail to re-instruct clearly, or fail to check that the employee has understood the re-instruction. So begin by reducing your feelings of frustration or irritation by consciously relaxing. Then, face the employee directly so that you can see each other clearly, but at a slight angle so that he (or she) does not feel confronted. Explain the problem.

Then, check from the other person's body language that he has grasped what you are saying. Are you receiving the clear nod of the head and eye contact that display understanding and agreement? Or are you getting the slight turn, glance away and dismissive gesture that signal that the employee resents what you are saying, or simply does not know what you are talking about? If the latter, you need to take action or explain your point more clearly.

What if staff need to be told clearly that they have done something wrong? It may be tempting to soften a disciplinary blow with gentle body language, but research has shown that a criticism accompanied by an apologetic smile or timid tone of voice creates resentment – employees think you are 'two-faced'. Instead, without getting angry, use body language appropriate to the occasion. Do not smile, do frown, do allow your voice to be serious. Such obviously disapproving body language will eventually lose its effect if it is your only way of behaving to staff, but will create the effect you want if you are the sort of manager who is usually even tempered and supportive.

Remember, finally, that once the disciplinary issue is over, it is important to let negative body language disappear – particularly if the employee's performance genuinely does improve. It can be tempting to keep a frosty air towards a 'culprit' for months afterwards, just to remind him of what might happen if he re-offends. But often all this does is to convince the employee nonverbally that he will never be able to get ahead in this particular company. And if he believes that, he will lose his motivation along with his job satisfaction.

How Can I Hire the Best Employee?

Many employers judge job applicants on their interview presentation. But there is a problem here: Interview performance has been shown to have a direct link with success only in those jobs that involve interview skills. In other words, if you choose an applicant because she (or he) is confident and extrovert, she will only do a good job for you if that job depends on her being confident and extroverted. If not then she may not be able to do the job at all!

One way round this which more and more companies are using is as follows. List the qualities you are looking for – practical, mental, emotional. Then, rather than asking an interviewee whether she has these qualities (to which question she will, of course, say yes), give her a series of practical tasks. As she performs each task, check her skill by observing her nonverbal approach; this will give you accurate information about how she would actually perform in practice.

Say that job success depends on an employee's being methodical and organized. At the interview, present her with a box of mixed stationery and ask her to reorganize it – then observe closely. Does she recognize which objects should be grouped together; does she use paper clips and folders to gather objects; does she pile things neatly and straighten corners; does she leave anything in the box and forget about it?

What if a job depends on an employee's working to a tight deadline or under stress? Set a straightforward practical task, such as filing, and add a deadline that puts the applicant under time-pressure so that she probably will not finish however fast she works. What you watch for is not whether she completes the task – though you do not tell the applicant this. Instead, notice whether she becomes less or more effective as the minutes tick away; whether she starts to drop things and apologize; whether she simply slows down until there is no chance of finishing; whether she rushes through inaccurately in order to get the job done.

Do you want an employee to be co-operative in her approach to work? In that case, get her doing a task in tandem with someone else, explaining clearly that it is working together that is the key skill you are looking for. It is amazing how, even given that instruction, different applicants will react in different ways. Does the candidate cut the other person out with hostile gestures and sharp tones in order to complete the job herself? Does she urge the other person on with an encouraging expression on her face and tone of voice? Does she smile and chat in a friendly fashion – but at the expense of the task in hand?

Using body language as your crucial test is an accurate and effective way of finding out who can do a job – and who only says she can!

How Can My Body Language Help Me Get the Job I Want?

So you are applying for a new post that will give you more of what you want – be it job satisfaction or hard cash! The first way body language can help is by showing you whether you really do want the job.

Nonverbal signals can give you high-quality information about your potential employer. As you take that pre-interview guided tour, look around at the architecture, the environment, the overall nonverbal style of the company (*see pages 42 and 44.*) Do the chipboard desks indicate a low-status company – if so, how do you feel about that? Do the partitioned workspaces hint that you need to work largely on your own to survive here – if so, will you fit in? Does the pace of people moving along corridors suggest that they are on tight deadlines – if so, are you happy working under pressure? If what you see puts you off, then in the long term you may not be happy with the job. If what you see excites you, then go for it.

As you move into the interview part of the selection procedure, use body language again to boost your self-presentation. For example, it is obviously a good thing to be confident during an interview; a steady approach makes you better able to demonstrate your real worth. So spend a moment calming yourself by taking a deep breath and letting it out, by tensing your muscles and then letting them 'flop'. Take up a confident position, sitting squarely on your chair rather than slumped to the back (which will make you look uninterested), perched on the front (which will make you look anxious), or angled unsymmetrically (which will make you look uncertain). Place your hands in your lap so that you will not be tempted to fidget nervously – though do not be afraid to make gestures to emphasize what you are saying.

As well as displaying confidence, also use the body language of approval. For research has shown that the body language patterns most likely to make interviewers feel positive about you are the ones that indicate you approve of them! So as they speak, acknowledge what they are telling or asking you: keep good eye contact, smile, nod when they say something you agree with.

Allow your body language – and your words – to reflect what you have seen in the company during your pre-interview tour. Of course there is no point in lying, verbally or nonverbally – in the end you either are or are not the right person for the job. But if you have spotted from existing employees' body language that being a people person is what is needed, mention your ability to get on with others and work as part of a team. Then let your body language demonstrate your extroversion as you interact with those you meet – interviewers and other staff alike. Show them, as well as tell them, that you are the right person for the job and that you deserve to go far!

As you reach the end of your interview, remember that recent research has shown that the last impression you make is the one that will stick most in interviewers' minds. So gather your belongings together efficiently, shake hands firmly, smile and make an unhurried exit.

Then wait for your letter of appointment...

3 ♥ Successful Social Life

How Can Body Language Help Me Build My Social Life?

Over 90 per cent of what people communicate to each other is nonverbal. So it goes without saying (as it were) that if you do not pay attention to body language, your relationships will always be less rewarding than they could be.

Body language first of all helps you understand people. Above and beyond the words, you can tell what others are really saying, interpret what they are trying to say, uncover what they are trying not to say. You can look at the way people stand, the gestures they make, the expressions on their faces, the way they speak – and use all that to build up a rounded picture of someone as a person, or a quick snapshot of him or her in a particular situation.

You can also adapt your own body language to be more successful with people. Rather than simply listening or talking, unaware of the impact you are making, you can start to choose to give people the body language messages you want to – that you are pleased to see them, that you are feeling bored, or that you want to see them again. Particularly, you can be aware of when you are making a bad impression, and put that right as soon as possible.

Recent research has developed a great deal of knowledge about body language in groups. So you can use body language particularly to analyse what is really happening under the surface during meals, at parties, when playing sport. And you can become much better able to make group events go well, because all the nonverbal elements such as the place, the time, the scene-setting will be right.

Your social life is important – so it's important to get it right. Whether in one-to-one friendships or in groups of friends, whether with perfect strangers or with people you have known for years, body language gives you extra tools with which to do just that.

What Really Happens When I Meet Someone New?

When you meet someone for the first time – at a party, in the pub, on the street – you become a video camera. You take a snapshot, with your eyes and ears. You scan, with eye movements so fast that they are practically unnoticeable, the most obvious details of the newcomer – height, weight, skin colour, clothes. Your ears respond to the first sounds of his (or her) voice, taking in accent, tone and volume levels. And within the first crucial ten seconds of even glimpsing someone, you use this snapshot to make an instant assessment. What a person looks like tells you how to think, feel and behave towards him.

If your new acquaintance is tall, for example, research shows that you will tend to think that he is both intelligent and successful. If this person is smaller than you are, on the other hand, you will be tempted to view him as ineffectual (if a man) or slightly helpless and in need of protection (if a woman). If the stranger is above normal weight, you may see him as easy-going, but lazy. If your new acquaintance is attractive – or at least, matches the current fashionable image of attractiveness in terms of physique and dress – then you are likely to expect him to be confident and at ease.

If she is female, you will expect her to be socially welcoming, and so you may smile and move forward; if he is male, you will expect him to be more confronting and assertive, so may stay back. And if the newcomer's gender is unclear – a man wearing kohl eyeliner or a woman with a masculine figure – then studies show that you will get confused, irritated and anxious.

Perhaps the most basic assessment you make about a new acquaintance concerns 'status'. In other words, is he more 'important' than you are? Some nonverbal status symbols in Britain at present are: being a man, being older, being expensively dressed, having a standard (i.e., southern) English accent. So, for example, if a newcomer is obviously much older than you, you will probably act as if he is also 'wiser', perhaps letting him speak first, being more likely to agree with him, nodding as he makes his points.

There is only one problem: These reactions to another person's nonverbal appearance are not only instinctive and instant. They are also very often quite inaccurate. Not all people above average weight are lazy. Not all beautiful people are necessarily confident.

And here is the twist, of course: While you are judging other people on their appearance, they, of course, are judging you on yours. The assumptions you make about others are just as likely to be the assumptions they make about you...

What Do I Do When I Begin an Interaction – with Different People?

First contact is often the most important part of any interaction. The moment you greet someone, you reveal your attitude, your mood – even your personality. You do this by five key things in your body language: your posture, your facial expression, your movements, your tone of voice, your touch. All these combine to give the person you greet a distinct impression of you. For example...

Are you giving the impression of formal respect – perhaps to a boss, or the bank manager? Formal body language is all about being direct, controlled but a little distant. So you may take up a straight posture, facing the other person head-on but standing back and keeping your distance. A formal smile is pleasant but brief, often with lips closed rather than the more informal smile that shows your teeth. A formal tone of voice is low, slow and steady, giving an impression of confidence and competence because it does not let any emotional insecurity show. And formal touch – though vital to create trust – is limited, often just an arm's-length handshake.

But say you are greeting a friend in the pub. Here your approach changes completely. You already know the other person, so your body language can be much more casual. You just glance briefly, give a 'greeting' nod and smile. You may not face the other person directly or touch in greeting, because the relationship is already established (unless of course, you are French, a nationality that shakes hands compulsively every time they pass each other in the street!). On the other hand, it is also much more acceptable to let your body language reveal your emotions, even your negative feelings. So you may well frown with anxiety, slam down your glass in frustration or let your tone of voice show just what a rotten day you have had.

Different again is greeting someone you want to build a close relationship with – perhaps a friend's new partner or a member of a new partner's family. Here you do not want to be formal, but cannot afford to be casual; you want to forge strong and positive links. You lean towards the other person to show you are interested. You smile with the genuine smile that reveals your teeth and wrinkles your eyes. You use open, 'inclusive' gestures that tell the other person that you want her (or him) to be part of your life. And you use touch to create and reinforce the link between you, with a double hand clasp, a lingering pat on the shoulder, a kiss on the cheek. Getting as close as you can, you forge a bond at the start that will make you feel good about each other for a long time to come.

What Is the Secret of Being a Good Listener?

A good listener is a mirror – not a blanket or a brick wall. Some people, the 'blankets', constantly interrupt the flow of the other person's conversation with their own nonverbal signals – shifting, blinking, looking away. The brick walls, on the other hand, give nothing back; they stand quiet and motionless, making no response, until the talker simply dries up and falls silent.

But if you are listening well, your body language is a mirror of what the other person is saying. So begin by using the 'mirrors' of the soul, the eyes, to look at the other person, showing your interest in him (or her) and his words. Do not worry if he looks away – he may have to in order to think – but keep your gaze on his face, and mark your visual interest further by making sure that the rest of your body is inclined in his direction too. Good listeners also tend to tilt their head slightly, because jaw angle actually affects the ability to hear better; so let your head naturally angle to one side.

Also, use the universal sign of acknowledgement, the nod of the head. An effective nod is usually hardly noticeable, but it is another kind of mirror, naturally happening at just the point where the speaker gets most animated – where he puts stress on a particular

vital word or where he gestures strongly to make a point. If the speaker then says something even more important, you may find yourself giving a longer, slower nod of the head, suggesting that you are taking him just that bit more seriously.

You can add to this message by picking up on what the other person is feeling and, in your role as 'mirror', reflecting it back to him. This does not mean howling with laughter if he merely smiles; but smiling when he laughs, taking on a sympathetic expression when he talks about something sad, frowning with empathetic irritation when he gets angry. These emotional reflections give the message 'I can feel some of what you are feeling. I understand.'

Good listening obviously involves asking questions. But a question thrown in when the speaker is not ready is worse than no question at all. So before you query, watch for the natural break, signalled by the speaker's slowing down, letting his voice rise or fall in pitch, looking directly at you as if appealing for a response, giving an open-palmed movement that says 'It's your turn now.'

In return, your question can be accompanied by a head tilt, a slight smile, a raise of the eyebrows: the body language that gives the reassuring message: 'I don't disagree with you ... I just want to know.' Then, as you reach the end of your question, hand back to the speaker with a direct look and that open-handed, turn-giving gesture mentioned before.

How Can I Really Involve Listeners in What I Am Saying?

Talking is not only about the words. When you speak, you also communicate through your body. And if you want to involve others in what you are saying, you need to use body language that involves them too.

Begin by letting your posture and expression show that you are aware of the other person. Turn fully towards her (or him); this tells her you are interested in making contact and allows her to get the most amount of information as you speak. Use wide 'inclusive' movements that say 'I want to involve you in what's happening.' And although you will regularly need to look away while speaking in order to think about what to say next, always re-establish contact with your listener by looking back at her at regular intervals.

The next step is to let your fingers do the talking. Effective speakers use gestures to communicate fully with their audience, emphasizing, explaining, clarifying – Italians, that most involving of nations, can actually become speechless if asked to sit on their hands! So become aware of the natural gestures you use and then make them clearer, more definite, more relevant to what you are saying.

You might use a 'baton' gesture. This is a downwards or sideways movement of the hand, so-called because it beats out the important points of your conversation just as a conductor's baton beats out key musical rhythms. You may use a 'metaphor' gesture, to draw out in the air a picture of what you really mean – curving your hands perhaps to indicate that you feel something is unified or complete, pushing your palms downwards if you are talking about a drop in noise or emotion. Or you may use 'punctuation' gestures to show that you have come to the end of a point; waving a hand with palm down to finish a statement, turning your hand palm up to invite the other person to talk for a while.

Also, use your voice to draw the listener in. Have a clear, confident tone that is not anxiously nasal, or breathless. Adopt a speed that is fast enough to keep up interest, but slow enough to be understandable. Use the rhythm of your voice to stress the words that are important to you in what you say. And remember that if you occasionally lower your voice just a fraction, or even pause for a moment, a person will automatically listen more carefully to you for the next few sentences.

Some speakers can say the most wonderful things – but their listeners feel alienated because their body language is static or rejecting. Using all your body skills to enthuse and include people will mean that they take what you say more seriously, and respond to it much more positively.

Can I Tell from Other People's Body Language What Sort of People They Are?

The answer to this question is both yes and no. If you try to judge someone from the shape of his (or her) hands or the position of his legs, you will almost always get it wrong. The uncontrollable, genetically inherited elements of a person's body, such as the shape of his hands, have no direct link with what kind of person he is. And short-term body language, such as temporary leg position, is so variable and flexible that it always has to be interpreted in the particular context in which you see it.

Some parts of a person's non-verbal appearance do reveal personality – those points that have been formed by past and repeated life experiences. Some schools of psychology hold that by as young as nine or ten years of age, human beings have postures and expressions which are personal to them and which reflect their habitual ways of moving.

For if a person regularly thinks and feels a particular way, and therefore consistently stands, moves or even grimaces in specific body patterns, then his body will naturally tend to fall back into those same patterns. So if you really want to understand someone else, look at his normal 'resting' posture, the one he falls back into naturally. Look at the spontaneous tilt of his head. Examine his facial lines, where decades of fleeting expressions have etched their most common expressions firmly into place. Notice his regular, repeated sequences of movement – the way he walks, sits or breathes. Get a rounded picture of someone's body patterns and you will get a rounded picture of his character.

For example, is the person you are with easy-going – is his natural posture relaxed? Is he at home with people – does he naturally turn his head towards you, seeking your company? Is he an energetic and alert individual – are his movements habitually direct, rhythmic and well-paced?

You can add further to your analysis, by actually 'trying on' another person's habitual body language. In doing so, you actually gain a deeper understanding of them.

Say, for example, someone has that permanent stoop, with neck thrust forward, that gives the condition of depression its name. Try slipping into that position – slumped body, head down, eyes dropped – and feel yourself become more pessimistic. Conversely, take on the position of someone who holds himself upright, with head held high and a slight smile on his face – and you will find yourself understanding his essential optimism.

Of course, a person's character and personality are revealed by their words – but, more than we think, someone's non-verbal actions will also tell us who he is.

What Can Others' Eye Movements Tell Me About Them?

You may have noticed that as a person thinks, his (or her) eyes move. A friend may gaze ahead at whatever interests him, or look at you when you are talking. But when he is talking – and has to think about what he is saying – he will often look away, and in different directions – upwards, sideways, downwards. If he looks upwards or downwards, he may well tilt his head in that direction too; if he looks sideways, he may angle his head to one side as he does so.

Research by U.S. psychologists Richard Bandler and John Grinder now seems to indicate that when someone's eyes move like that, it shows that he is thinking in particular ways. To understand this, first remember that the two senses that we, as humans, mainly use are those of sight and hearing. We not only see and hear things; we also think in pictures and in sounds. (If you question that, try remembering first what your front door looks like, and secondly what your front door key sounds like as you put it in the lock; you will be able to recall these things, however vaguely, as a picture and a sound.)

Bandler and Grinder suggest that if a person looks upwards, then he is thinking about a sight; he has a picture of something in his head, is visualizing it in his mind's eye. If he glances to the side, he is thinking about a sound; he is maybe remembering a remark someone passed, or some music he is fond of, and is experiencing it in what we might call 'the mind's ear'. Further, if someone consistently looks in one direction – for example, upwards – that means that he thinks mainly in pictures and makes visual images of what he is thinking about. It also means that he is likely to remember what he sees very fully, that he will have a vivid, visual imagination and that he is likely to be good at things that require a strong visual sense. Further research suggests that the mind's eye can be used to recall early memories and even aid spelling (*see page 12*).

If someone tends to look mainly sideways, that indicates that he thinks mainly about what he hears. He is likely to remember best what he has heard, will be able to imagine sounds and words very clearly and is likely to be good at things that need a strong sense of sound or rhythm.

The research on which these ideas are based is new but exciting. Trained workers in the field claim to be able to map people's thought processes in some detail and with some accuracy. Without that training, you cannot really tell what people are thinking about second to second – though of course you can always ask when you see them glancing away.

What you can do, though, is start to get an insight about the way people experience the world. Take that friend mentioned at the start of this section; is he sight-orientated, or sound-orientated, a looker or a listener? And what does all this mean about the sort of person he is?

Lookers have a good visual sense and may need to see you in order really to relate. Listeners love music and all kinds of sound; they often have a good sense of rhythm. If you are chatting to a friend about something that happened, a looker will need you to build a picture that he can see in his mind's eye. The listener, on the other hand, will not need any descriptions but will enjoy the telling of the tale itself, a blow-by-blow account of what happened, when and in what order.

If it comes to buying presents, remember whom you are buying for. Your looker friend will want his gift beautifully wrapped, and will welcome anything that looks good and has visual style. Your listener friend will go into ecstasies over a record, or spoken-word books featuring the voices of great actors, but will not actually worry about the visual presentation. He will not even care too much if you wrap your gift in a brown paper bag!

How Can I Spot that I Am Boring People – and What Should I Do If I Am?

Unless you are being incredibly dull, then it may be quite difficult to spot that you are being boring. For it is not really socially acceptable for other people to admit they feel uninterested, or to show clear signs of boredom. People try to neutralize their body language so that others will not be offended by their reaction.

Perhaps the initial thing to be aware of, then, is whether the person opposite you is looking blank. She (or he) may go very still, stop making gestures, stop moving as she listens to you – all to hide her irritation and frustration. The other reason that a bored companion might suddenly go still and blank-faced is that in conversation, tiny movement signals such as smiles and nods are a listener's way of encouraging the speaker to go on and say more. If the person you are with does not actually want you to say more, then she will naturally cut down on those signals.

On the other hand, a bored person can move even more than usual – for comfort. People under stress have been shown to reduce tension by minute body shifts, which are possibly a comforting reminder of when, as children, we were rhythmically rocked by our mother's motions. Feet movements can also be interpreted as 'escape' movements, where the body tries to flee but cannot. If you see 'feet flurries' along with a body leaning towards the door or an unconscious turn of the head towards the exit, then you may have good reason to suspect that your companion simply wants to be gone!

What can you do? First, check if the other person's boredom is because something else, somewhere else, looks more interesting to her. If it is not actually you that is off-putting, but the view in the mirror behind you that is attractive, then move so that you alone are in the other person's line of sight. Shift so that your body is blocking her off from all distractions. Then reach out and touch her, perhaps reclaiming her attention by saying her name – the single sound that adult humans respond to most readily.

Or, allow your companion to do some of the talking. Is she giving you 'turn-demanding' signals – looking intently at you, nodding rapidly to hurry you up, taking a breath as if to speak as soon as you slow down? If so, be democratic. Bring your sentence to a close, ask a question about your listener's thoughts, and let her have her turn. You may find that her boredom signals instantly disappear!

How Can I Tell If People Really Find My Jokes Funny?

Amusement affects the whole of a person's body. It stimulates every organ in a way that has been described as 'stationary jogging', exercising the face, neck, shoulders, stomach and diaphragm. It reduces blood-pressure, increases the amount of oxygen in the blood, lowers the heart rate, boosts the immune system, even stimulates the body's natural painkillers, beta-endorphins. Laughter is, in fact, the best medicine.

What occurs on the surface of the body during amusement is just as dramatic. The impact inside almost always makes a person move around, even if only slightly. If very amused, he (or she) will shake with laughter. His breathing will quicken and he will often gasp for breath. He may even reach out as if for support to the person next to him. He will change colour, turning red because the amusement has expanded the blood vessels close to the surface of his skin.

If someone responds to a joke you tell as strongly as described above, then you can be certain that you have hit home. But what if the response is a little more low key? People do fake amusement, so as not to upset the joke-teller. How can you spot when someone is faking for you?

The main sign of real amusement, the one that a person just cannot fake, is the genuinely amused smile. A real smile comes quickly. It is synchronized with the joke to within 1/48th of a second, or sometimes even slightly before it, as the listener's mind makes the final leap ahead of the last syllable of the punch line. A real smile is symmetrical, equal on both sides of the face; it comes quickly and fades slowly. It curves upwards and brings into play the lines that run from the corner of the nose to the corner of the mouth (the naso-labial folds). It also involves the eyes, which crinkle slightly as the muscles around them respond to the smile.

No one can fake any of these movements, of mouth or of eyes; they are not under conscious control. So a faked smile comes slowly, dies away slowly, and is slightly imbalanced, as if one side of the face is aiming for a positive response while the other side is not too sure. A faked smile tends to be oblong rather than curved, because the smile muscles along the naso-labial folds are not really being used. And the eye muscles are not fully brought into play – which is why the cold, villainous smile of the movie 'baddie' never reaches his eyes.

Should you catch any of these signs of a false response, you may want to change your line in jokes – or tell them to a more appreciative listener!

What Are the Nonverbal Signs of a Really Good Friendship?

When you first make friends with someone, it is a bit like love without the sex. Adrenalin rushes through your body, your heart beats a little faster than usual, you feel a tingle inside, albeit a gentle and totally unsexual tingle. Do not worry. These physical reactions are perfectly normal – they are signs that you are getting on well with another person.

From the outside, you will also be displaying your enthusiasm. You will greet each other energetically, sometimes almost with yells of appreciation. You will use each other's names a lot. You will show off, flicking your hair back to show your 'good side'; raising your voice a little louder to make a point. And to show each other that you care, you will take all the nonverbal signs of liking and magnify them – looking at each other more than usual, smiling more than usual, nodding more than usual. The more you both do this, the more you will both feel appreciated and feel good about each other.

You will also want to be close to your friend – literally as well as emotionally. So you will stand close, face directly, reach out and touch – seemingly to emphasize a point, but actually to signal how close you are. You will 'match' in a whole variety of nonverbal ways – picking up each other's accents, dancing in the same style, laughing at the same jokes, wearing the same clothes, not only to strengthen the feeling between you but also to show other people your bond – and to warn them off muscling in on the friendship.

Interestingly, when you are more sure of the relationship, many of these signs die away – and there is no need to worry if they do. Your body language becomes far more like that of a long-established married couple. You greet each other with pleasure, but calmly. You are more at ease sitting side by side rather than opposite, now that you do not need to see each other's faces in order to tell what each of you is thinking. You talk less, and less excitedly, now that you do not need to exchange words to know how each of you is feeling. You smile less, laugh less, call each other by name less – because you are already close and do not need these signals to bind you together.

But despite the fact that you may seem more distanced, you are, if anything, more close. You walk along together, totally in step. You and your friend will both move to cross the street at the same time, without noticeable signals. You reach for your drink at the same moment, shift position at the same second. When you reach this stage with someone, you do not need to try any more. Your friendship is deep, and potentially long-lasting.

When Friends Visit, How Can the Environment Make or Break the Evening?

To really enjoy themselves, people need to be able to be themselves without tension. But they will find it difficult to do that if the environment gives the opposite message. So while antique furniture and cut-glass will impress, they will also make it more difficult for guests to be informal. Ornaments that say 'look but don't touch', elegant furniture that keeps people on the edge of their seats, pristine carpets in pure white: all these are death to relaxation. Instead, opt for deep comfy sofas in deep, stain-resistant hues.

Other ways of helping people to relax include the use of colour, heating and light. Warm colours in a mildly heated room will encourage people to sit back and move slowly rather than huddle forwards and talk quickly as they will do if they feel chilly. A too-warm room, though, has been shown to make people irritated and argumentative – so unless you want a fierce discussion during the evening, keep an eye on the thermostat!

Be wary too of bright lighting, which encourages brisk body language totally at odds with relaxed friendly chat; and of lighting that is just too dim – within 20 minutes of lowering the lights during

one research study, conversation had stopped entirely and the subjects were mostly interested in catnapping!

Once relaxed, people then want to relate as easily as they can to the others in the room. So do all you can to create an environment that will make everyone feel included. If any chairs are 'out on a limb', move them into the main group. Avoid high, formal chairs mingled with lower and more informal seating, which will leave the occupants feeling stranded above or below the conversation. Place chairs at angles with each other rather than on opposite sides, which can make people feel antagonistic towards each other – one reason why arguments tend to happen at the meal table more often than when people are using the 'angled' seating usually found in a living room.

Do not think, though, that people who are in close proximity will naturally interact more positively. If the space they actually have to sit in is actually too small, as happens when two people have to squash together on a cramped sofa, then they will go on the defensive. They will cross their arms and hunch their shoulders to protect their own personal space – and this will not make for relaxed conversation. And if the seating is too deep and soft, then people may feel themselves tilting back or sliding towards others, and this lack of control will also make them feel wary.

Finally, do not forget sound. Music that is too loud will keep people from talking and thinking. Music that is too slow may simply send them to sleep. But music that acts as a background to interaction – providing a slow, soft, relaxing setting that does not intrude – will add to all the other nonverbal scene-setting you have done and help to create an enjoyable evening.

How Should I Use Body Language When Friends Come Round for a Meal?

When your evening with friends includes food, then as far as body language is concerned, it doesn't matter if it is pasta and salad or a five-course banquet. If guests are to enjoy themselves, you need to move them through a series of distinct phases.

In order to enjoy food, people need to relax – otherwise their stomach muscles will close up and the digestive juices will not flow. So the first part of the evening ideally provides time and space for people to wind down – often from a busy day – and also get ready to eat. So you may allow at least half an hour between people arriving and eating for them to relax; sit them down comfortably on soft seating, perhaps with gentle music; you might offer drinks and snacks designed to stimulate the digestive juices.

There is another purpose to this pre-meal chat: Studies have shown that if people feel insecure with others, then they lose their appetite. By allowing time before a meal for the group to chat, you make it less likely that this will happen. And it is a good idea, if someone indicates by her (or his) body language that she is not joining in, to chat for a few minutes, putting her at ease until she seems to be more comfortable.

Then, you can move on to the meal. There is a purely biological reason here why you ideally move to a higher table and more upright chairs. Simply, it is easier to enjoy and digest food if the body is more upright and therefore the stomach and gut are not squashed by sitting. You will probably find, too, that seating people in a more upright way, closer together, raises their energy levels; they may start talking more quickly, allowing their voices to rise, smiling more.

As the food settles, slowly the group will become quieter and slower. As with any animal, humans tend to become drowsy after eating, because all our energy is going into the serious business of digestion. At this point you may want to allow people to leave their upright chairs and collapse onto the most relaxing seating you have, to the accompaniment of really slow and soporific music. Conversation may calm down; people want to be quieter. At this point, if your friends followed their animal instincts, they would simply slide into a horizontal position and fall asleep.

In fact, because everyone but you has to go home, it is best to give people an extra burst of energy to allow them to travel safely. The final ritual drink of coffee not only offsets any possible negative effects of drowsiness on the driver, but livens everyone up so that they can cope with the journey home.

How Can I Say No to a Friend without Alienating Him?

Your best friend wants to borrow your car for the weekend. You may think that he (or she) will dislike you if you refuse.

This can happen. But problems usually only occur because you are anxious about these possibilities or because you are irritated at your friend for putting you in this situation. In short, friendships get chipped away at the edges not because the signals read 'I'm saying no' but because they read 'I'm saying no – and that makes me feel bad about you.'

One danger is this: When your friend makes his request, you feel defensive because you feel bad about refusing. This shows as you unconsciously pull back, turn away, stare angrily, block off your body with your arms, shake your head, let your voice rise irritably. The problem is that all these signals seem to say that you are angry; they are the same kind of signs that apes use to reject unwelcome contact from others. No wonder that, however amicable your words, your friend feels completely rejected for 'only asking'.

Another possibility is that your body language signals to your friend that you feel guilty about refusing. You give a repentant smile, grimace apologetically, hunch your shoulders and look away in embarrassment. But then an interesting thing happens: You expect this body language to improve matters, to make your friend feel better about your refusal. But in fact the opposite happens; your friend gets irritable. He does this because your body language signals of guilt are similar to body language signals of admitting wrong and inviting punishment. At the very point that you want to make amends, your friend may feel an almost irresistible compulsion to hit back.

The secret of refusing a request without causing trouble is to combine clear 'no' signals with clear approval signals. In other words, you need to signal nonverbally as well as verbally that you will not do what your friend wants, but that you do want to stay friends.

So be definite about your refusal. Assertiveness trainers, who are usually past masters at the art of effective body language, suggest that you stand straight and say a clear and direct 'no', while looking the other person full in the eye and shaking your head to make the point clearly. If your friend argues, simply repeat your refusal with the same body language – but stay calm, do not look defensive, do not look apologetic.

At the same time, signal friendship. Once your refusal has been accepted, then smile, use a warm tone of voice, add a quick touch – a tap on the shoulder or a pat on the arm – to reassure. If you can indicate by your response that you are saying 'no' to the request but are not rejecting the person, then even if there is bad feeling it probably will not last.

Some People Just Seem to Find It Easy to Get Chatting to Others Wherever They Go. How Do They Do That?

People who are able to 'get chatting' to others, perhaps on a train or in a bus queue, have a special secret. They use their body language skills to let the other person feel secure enough to start talking and to keep talking.

So people who nonverbally seem safe have the best chance of making contact. They look safe: little old ladies find it easier to strike up a conversation than do large muscular men. They dress 'safely': standard casual clothes give off more safety signals than do black leather and chains. They act safely: standing quietly at a bus stop in the middle of the day provides more chance of making contact than rolling up to the same bus stop at midnight in an inebriated state.

People who get talking easily use friendly body language. They are not bowed down with unhappy expressions or nervous twitches. They walk in an easy manner. They do not use protective signals, such as arms across the body and hunched shoulders; or 'elsewhere' signals such as absent-minded gazes or thoughtful frowns. They often have a naturally happy expression, suggesting that they will be fun to be with as well as safe – one Brazilian study shows that people who smile are always viewed more positively than those who keep a straight face.

The way these people make contact is also part of the secret. Their first step is automatically to look around at everyone they meet; they simply cannot help scanning a room as they enter it, glancing across at the other people in their train compartment, making eye contact in a queue. Then they follow a nonverbal 'safety routine' which allows them, or the people they look at, to withdraw if either is unhappy at what is happening. So if others do not hold eye contact because they feel wary, then the successful social-izer does not take things further. Only if the eye contact is returned confidently do things proceed to a second step – another glance across to establish interest on both sides.

Next there is a small smile, a signal even in the ape world that one means no harm. Is the smile returned? Again, if not, then nothing more happens. But if so, then perhaps it is time for a word or two – choosing a safe neutral topic such as why the train is delayed. These 'excuse' comments are made in a light, throw-away tone which does not expect a reply. But if one is given, then both partners smile more broadly, move more energetically, actu-ally shift noticeably closer together to show how well they are getting on.

The conversation has begun, the contact has been made. They will probably keep talking all the way from London to Glasgow!

What Are the Problems I Might Encounter If I Try to Turn Work Relationships into Social Relationships?

Most people make friends at work, but it does have its dangers – even if you never actually reveal your innermost secrets. The dif-ferent kinds of body language that being friends and being work-mates involve may mean that at some point you feel uneasy but you don't know why.

The reason is this: The body language of colleagues is designed to work in a professional context. You have to get things done, not gossip or get emotional. So body language develops to keep you at a distance.

You approach mainly within the social zone of 3.6 – 1.2 m (12 – 4 ft), only sometimes within the personal zone of less than 1.2 m (4 ft), rarely within the intimate zone of less than 45 cm (18 in). You will keep barriers between you, either literally with a desk or chair, or with protective movements such as an arm's-length handshake. You will keep emotional barriers up by making sure that you do not show your feelings too much. You will make sure that your expression and voice do not distract others from the job in hand.

But then you go out to the wine bar together or you end up dancing in a group at the Christmas party. For that short time, in a social setting, the rules are different and all your body language shifts. You do not keep your distance, but huddle together on a pub bench. You smile broadly, you nod, you exchange friendly touches – all signs that you like each other. You do not hold back on the emotions, but laugh or cry in a way that in nonverbal terms is actually designed to make you feel closer to each other. It does not seem strange; it is what enjoying yourself with other people is all about.

Until the morning. If you then try to take the body language of the wine bar back into the workplace, you can find yourself feeling bad without knowing why. A colleague – male or female – moves closer than you want, and suddenly you feel uneasy. Two employees suddenly start giggling, heads together, when in a meeting.

Your boss, who was so informal last night in the pub, suddenly seems uneasy at being greeted with a smile and a nudge. What is happening?

Not unnaturally, bodies are getting confused. They are halfway between friendship mode and work mode, so that everyone feels uncomfortable; what they want is one thing or another. And in fact, one way or another, your body language will find a balance. One possibility is that everyone will fairly quickly switch back to work mode and the status quo will be restored; you will make sure not to socialize with each other again except on very rare occasions.

Or, some of you at least will find a way to mix work and pleasure. You will meet out of office hours, but you will take care to use one kind of behaviour before five o'clock and another kind afterwards. To get the best of both worlds, you will learn not to distract yourselves from work by using social body language. At the same time, of course, you will learn not to inhibit your social life by using the body language of work!

How Can I Survive at a Party Where Everyone Already Seems to Know Everyone Else?

You arrive at a party only to find you are a stranger. Everyone seems to be locked in conversation with everyone else, and you are the wallflower. What can you do?

Begin by using your body language skills to identify groups that are actually open to new members. If people are standing in a tightly packed group, shoulder to shoulder, with most people adding comments in confident, loud voices and lots of synchronized laughter, then almost certainly they are already good friends. They may react with surprise and even some negativity if you try to squeeze in.

If, on the other hand, people are standing fairly far apart, talking in turn with quieter voices and not much movement, this is more likely to be a temporary group; their posture and their conversation patterns are literally leaving space for new members to join in.

Even so, these people will already have a sense of identity as a group. You will raise hackles if you simply barge in and start talking. There is, in fact, a clear nonverbal etiquette for joining such a group; follow it and you will have a smooth ride.

Use body language to 'knock' before entering. Stand just outside the group, but very close; almost certainly someone will glance round, spot you and, if you smile reassuringly, will shift to let you in.

Ease gently into the gap. Then stand quietly and watch what is going on around you. You will notice that there is a nonverbal pattern to what the group is doing. One way or another they will be 'matching' each other's posture, gestures or voice levels. Perhaps a number of them are holding their glasses in the same way; perhaps when one person takes a drink, the others do too. To succeed in the group you need to match these nonverbal patterns. If everyone nods, nod too; smile along with other people; groan when they groan at a bad joke. Matching in this way will reassure the group that you are not trying to barge in or take over. So match, even if only for a few minutes.

When you are ready to join in the conversation, again watch the nonverbal cues. There may be a sort of 'pass the parcel' game whereby one person takes the lead, then bounces the conversation to another, who passes it back or passes it on. If you want to speak, start catching the eye of the person who seems to be taking the lead. Keep looking at her (or him) with the raised eyebrows and tilted head that nonverbally says 'Can I have a turn please?' When she feels you are sufficiently accepted, she will pass the parcel to you, winding up her comment and making the 'turn-taking' open-palm gesture that shows you now have the floor.

Take your chance and say something. As you do, look round at everyone in a friendly fashion, to make them feel included in what you are saying. But do not hog the attention; 'pass the parcel' back after a few sentences. You will get your chance to speak again.

Who Is Top of the Pecking Order in My Group?

In every group of people there is some sort of pecking order. This is not to do with being in charge; the team coach, the hostess or some other kind of formal leader is not always at the top of the pecking order. But all humans, in groups, sort themselves out into a hierarchy, with some people being seen as more important because they do things that the group value. Perhaps these people are older, perhaps they have been group members for longer, or perhaps they simply score goals more often.

The pecking order can change, according to what a group is doing. So extrovert Sally may be top of the pecking order when you are at the pub; everyone laughs at her jokes and jumps to it when she suggests getting the drinks in. But when it comes to buying a car, all of a sudden introvert Tom comes into his own because Tom is the world's expert on how to avoid buying a rustbucket; in that situation, everyone listens quietly and respectfully, including Sally.

Most people are never aware of the pecking order in their particular group, but body language always reflects that order. Automatically, consistently, unconsciously people will behave slightly differently towards those 'above' them in the pecking order than they do towards those 'on their level' or 'below' it.

So how can you spot the pecking order in a group you are in? Begin by looking at position: Who sits at the focal point of the group? Who takes up the central position? This person does not have to sit in the highest or largest chair, but his (or her) spot will be the one that draws attention when you walk in the room. After a while, every other chair will end up slightly turned towards it.

What about priority? Who goes first, through a door or in the coffee round? Who is asked first what he would like to eat, or where he would like to go?

What about verbal dominance? Who speaks first, longest, and holds the group's attention most? It may be the person with the loudest voice, or it may be a quiet and retiring individual. But when he speaks, there will be absolute silence.

Who is able to persuade? Whose ideas seem to meet with approving nods and smiles rather than consideration or dubious glances? Who is it who gets copied if he wears something new, buys something different, starts going to a new place?

You may need to watch for a while, as pecking order shifts from one person to the other over the course of hours or even just a few minutes. But by analysing just who in your group is number one in any situation, you will gain real insight into how you and your friends get on with each other, and how you all interact together as a group.

What Are Group 'Roles' and How Can I Spot Them?

A social group is a bit like a sports team; different people play in different positions. This all happens largely unconsciously. People take up roles in a group, act out various parts, fulfil distinct functions. For example...

Most groups have a resident clown. It is usually a man in a mixed sex group; he makes jokes, plays the fool and does not mind being silly in order to have fun. He moves more freely than everyone else, and often gets down on the floor with the dog or the children. And when shoulders are up, voices are raised and everyone's body language shrieks 'stress' or 'fight', the clown is the one who punctures the tension so that everyone falls about laughing.

The 'earth mother' – only occasionally an 'earth father' – is usually the hostess. She is in the kitchen when you arrive and may spend most of the time bringing cups of tea or slices of cake rather than sitting down and talking to you. She will hug a lot, touch a lot, smile a lot – all approving and reassuring signals. She may also often look worried or frowning because she is always rushing round looking after people.

The 'vamp' can be male or female, and hardly ever means any harm. The female version cares about her appearance more than other women in the group do, and may wear makeup when the others do not. Both male and female vamps talk at length to members of the opposite sex, looking deeply into their eyes in the same way real lovers do, murmuring in soft, low voices, reaching out and touching others.

The 'misery' is miserable. His body language runs through a number of negative emotions, usually a mixture of sadness and anger. Perhaps he sits slumped in his chair a lot of the time; perhaps he is always going for long, angry walks; perhaps he often turns up ill or having had an accident. The misery often needs looking after, having a special chair to sit in, eating special food, going to bed early.

The 'talent' often does have a real gift – maybe for playing a musical instrument, for writing or for working with her hands. She often talks little, just sitting and watching other people. But when she demonstrates her talent – starting to play, sing, make something or perform – then she is always the centre of attention.

Can you spot, from these body language descriptions, whether the groups you mix in contain people playing these roles? And if so – who plays what?

What Can Go Wrong for a New Person Joining an Old, Established Group?

You go with a group of friends for a meal. Two of them bring along their friends, people you have not met before. Then a strange thing happens: One of the newcomers fits in and the other doesn't. It does not seem to have anything to do with personality; both people seem very pleasant. But somehow the group welcomes one of them and totally ignores the other.

What is happening here is this: Each of the newcomers is behaving in a slightly different way – and one of them does not quite fit with what is happening. Any existing group of friends has a way of interacting that is theirs alone. It is down not so much to the group's topics of conversation as their patterns of behaviour. They hug every time they meet, or never, ever touch. They sit in one particular corner of the pub, or they stand at the bar. They wear jeans, or they wear business suits.

Newcomers can easily pick up on the verbal side of group behaviour. They can listen to what is said, then match their statements, questions and opinions to the mood of the group. But newcomers may not be aware of the group's nonverbal rules. And, not knowing these rules, they can make mistakes.

If newcomers carry on as they normally do, then the chances are good that they will not follow the group's way of doing things. They may sit down without checking out the normal seating arrangement. They may smoke during the meal rather than after. There is nothing wrong in doing these things; it just is not what the group does.

But such actions can arouse the strongest and most unexpected negative feelings. The nonverbal message is that such people are different; the unspoken fear is they might try to influence the group to do things their way. There will be a sense of insecurity and defensiveness, without anyone even knowing why; ranks will close, and the newcomers will be excluded.

If you are part of an existing group and a newcomer joins, you can make it easier for him (or her). First, become aware of what your nonverbal rules are: about clothes, about greeting, about sitting, about eating and drinking, about talking, about 'pairing off', about saying goodbye – in fact, about every aspect of your group's behaviour. Then, give the newcomer a fighting chance by mentioning things in advance, or pointing out, supportively rather than challengingly, if he gets it wrong. People want to fit in; they will almost always change to suit.

If you are a newcomer, the secret is to watch from the sidelines for quite a while. If you take the time to identify, learn and copy the group rules, then eventually you will be accepted. So look and listen for the nonverbal patterns. What do you wear? Is it OK for the men to talk to the women? When is going home time? Then, do what everyone else does, just until they feel safe with you. Sooner or later you will be talked to, listened to, taken seriously, allowed to do things your way – because you are now one of the crowd.

How Does Body Language Help a Sports Team to Be a Real 'Team'?

The initial step in any team's success is this: Members need to start thinking of themselves as a unit, a whole, a group that acts as one. Clever team leaders know that body language is often the key.

For example, there is clothing that makes all the members look roughly the same, and also makes them look different from the other teams. There may even be a certain hair style – very short for the Boy Scouts, pony tails for the cheerleaders. This common 'look' not only helps members to identify with their own group and feel special but also to develop a sense of competition with other groups.

Next, the team may do lots of physical activities together – the workout, the training session, the drill or the rehearsal. This not only gets them feeling physically good, full of adrenalin, on a high when they are with each other; it also gets them deliberately 'matching' each other – and when humans start moving in synchrony, they naturally start acting as a unit.

As team members start to feel closer to each other, they may also start to reveal this by unconscious or informal matching. Without realizing it, team members may start to take on the same ways of moving, picking up each other's accents, developing 'in phrases', using special handshakes when they meet.

As the time comes to face opponents, the clever team leader will next start to channel the natural physical energy that the team members feel into the game or competition. Perhaps they will start singing aggressive chants, clapping or stamping their feet – yet more rhythmic matching movement that brings the group together, gets their adrenalin going ready for the challenge and concentrates their minds by focusing their body movements. By the time they are due to 'perform', this skilful use of nonverbal elements should mean that each team member is physically and mentally in tune with all the others, physically and mentally focused on success.

And when that success comes, the most basic reward also involves body language. The first thing that usually happens, when a goal is scored or a point gained, is that all the other team members come up and touch the scorer – the most basic way humans have not only of making another person feel good but also of creating a feeling of closeness to each other.

As they return to the locker room, everyone's happy and relaxed body language shows that they are at ease with each other. What started as a number of individuals has, by skilful use of body language, turned into a cohesive and united team.

How Can I Make a Party Go With a Swing?

If your aim is movement rather than talk, dancing rather than chat, mixing and mingling rather than sitting and interacting, then you need to create a very particular nonverbal atmosphere for your next party.

The traditional guidelines for organizing a party actually get it right: You clear the decks and put away anything valuable, not only to protect your property but also so that people feel able to move more freely, to use open, friendly gestures, to take up lots of space when they move. You provide hard chairs so that people do not sit down for long and have to keep moving and mixing with each other. You turn the lighting down – when you do this, people stop talking. And you turn the music up so that even if guests do talk, they simply are not able to hear each other.

You invite far more people to the party than you believe the space can hold – not only because, as everyone knows, only half the people you invite will turn up! You do it because, up to a certain point, the more friends there are in a room the better those friends are likely to feel about what is happening. For being together with lots of 'safe others' is very stimulating to human beings: adrenalin surges, heart rates rise, sociable touch stimulates and everyone feels positive.

It is important if you are running the party, though, also to keep an eye out for the nonverbal signals that show people are not enjoying themselves. Watch for people standing tensely with their backs to the wall; people who are trying to shut out the sound with slightly hunched shoulders; people who are trying to shut out what they see with downward glances and vague stares; people standing side by side, not talking but gazing out vaguely into the room. Swoop down, carry these people off and introduce them to a small group that is interacting fairly quietly, where they can unwind and find a number of different people to talk to.

As the evening continues you will want to raise the energy level. Make sure the music becomes faster and louder, which will have this effect. Get lots of guests dancing together, because if people move in synchrony they feel good about each other. Do not add too much alcohol, because although at first it may seem to energize people, in the end it may make them either aggressive or sleepy.

As the party begins to end, lower the energy level. Otherwise, after all the excitement and exercise people can feel just too stimulated to sleep. The tradition of ending an evening with soft, low music not only provides an opportunity to snuggle and cuddle, it also allows people to wind down gradually, to start to calm down and get ready to drift off home.

How Can I Get On Socially When I Meet My Partner's Friends?

Is there any occasion more nerve-wracking than being introduced to 'the crowd'? Will they disapprove? Will they be jealous? Will they hate you so much that your partner leaves you?

These are not silly fears. Old established groups can feel threatened by new members, as explained on page 110. And the threat seems greater to them if the newcomer has the weapons of sex and love with which she (or he) may actually lure away an existing member. The group will not feel able to say anything to you, but they may well reveal their defensiveness nonverbally by greeting you with a flat, false smile and handshake while they greet your partner with enthusiastic hugs; by leaving you isolated at one end of the dinner table while they cluster up the other end; by laughing, joking and touching each other even more enthusiastically than usual, just to make the point that their group is special and you are not part of it.

Quite naturally, your body language will also go on the defence. In return you will hang on to your partner literally and metaphorically, holding his (or her) hand or arm, demanding the deep eye contact of established lovers, talking in soft, low loving tones – all aimed to show that you are a couple and that no one else can intrude. Alternatively, if you are feeling annoyed, your mouth may

become tight or sulky, your voice loud or aggressive; then at some point you may well find that everyone else falls silent, leaving your strident tones rising into a secretly triumphant room.

You can largely avoid this scenario from hell if you are aware of the nonverbal undercurrents. Remember that first impressions matter. Underdress rather than overdress because then you may not impress but you certainly will not threaten anyone. If you can find out what the 'group style' is, dress to that, whether it be jeans, dinner jackets, or first one then the other. Gauge makeup or after-shave carefully; if you are the only one wearing them at breakfast, you may be history by the end of the day!

Do not cling to your partner; it hints that your long-term agenda is to take her over completely. Instead, however hard it is, mix. Which of the friends shows, by eye contact and smiles, that she is prepared to be welcoming? Chat to her first; once you have got her on your side, work your way steadily round the circle, spending time with everyone. Leave until last any who seem a little antagonistic, shown by the fact that they do not seem able to look at you, or that they talk to you in flat, expressionless voices.

Once you have made contact with everyone, then act just as you would if you were trying to join any group. Be friendly and approachable. Notice what the nonverbal group norms are and follow them (*see page 107*). Use helpful body language: nothing is more guaranteed to endear you than getting the drinks in, clearing the dishes or doing the washing up.

Finally, steer very clear of anyone who seems attracted to you. If someone sits close, looks into your eyes or 'accidentally' touches your hand, then turn your attention elsewhere. These are all signals that they are sexually attracted to you. Jealousy from your partner or someone else's is the last thing you need in this situation!

How Can Body Language Help Me Realize When a Friendship Is at an End?

Friendships do end, either because of bad feeling or just because you have grown apart. Yet people rarely 'end' a friendship with the same dramatically displayed emotions with which they often end a partnership. So how can you tell what is happening?

Look first at the more obvious nonverbal signals: You are phoning each other less often, spending less time with each other. Your friend is busy more often. Months rather than weeks go by without contact. These things can happen simply because you are both busy, so look next at what happens when you are together.

Where do you meet? If it used to be at each other's homes and it is now a restaurant, then this may be a sign that one of you feels less willing to allow the other into his (or her) personal space. You may feel uneasy about the relationship and this reveals itself in unease about having your space invaded. If the two of you used to meet in a restaurant and now it is always with a group at a film, then maybe this is a nonverbal statement that you do not actually want to interact one-to-one anymore.

If you do meet as a pair, do you have as much attention for each other as you used to? Do you find it difficult to maintain eye contact? Do you find your friend's expression 'glazing over' as you talk? Are there lots of 'escape' movements, tapping of fingers or flicking of feet, going on? Are the pauses longer than the talking – or is one of you doing all the talking now while the other one does all the listening? All these signals suggest that at least one of you does not feel the same emotional bond as before.

What if the feelings are actually negative? Have you ever looked up from your meal to find a fleeting expression of something nasty cross someone else's face? These 'leakages', as psychologists call them, happen when a person's real feelings of anger, mockery or even fear unconsciously escape and show for just a fraction of a second.

If you see this, then you may well want to end the friendship. The most usual approach is the initial one mentioned above, of simply seeing less and less of someone. Or, if you do not mind some bad feeling, you can deliberately use body language to bring things to an end. Increase all your negative signals, lose attention, lose eye contact, fidget and seem bored. Your friend will get the message, consciously or unconsciously – and you will both then 'forget' to make another arrangement to meet again.

What Is a Goodbye Ritual and Why Does It Matter?

Unlike animals, human beings do not just walk away when they lose interest. They want to meet again, so they want to part on good terms; breaking contact is so significant that, every time, there is a little ritual to accompany it. So when you say end a conversation and say your goodbyes to someone, you go through a whole series of body language movements to bring things to an end.

'byeeee'

The first stage is to signal to the other person that you want her (or him) to finish what she is saying – so that you can go. You might find yourself nodding more often and more quickly, a sign of agreement that carries the hidden message that since she has convinced you, she can be silent now. Maybe you find yourself catching the other person's eye, or half opening your mouth to speak, in the conversational signal that means – 'I want to take a turn; please stop.'

When she has stopped, and you have her attention, you use your turn not to speak but to signal that you want to go. You turn slightly away, look towards the direction you will be going, maybe indicate that direction by a totally unconscious wave of your hand, look down towards your watch as if you are signalling that you have run out of time.

Your companion will almost certainly respond. She will 'match' what you are doing, copying your look away, turning towards the exit too, signalling that she has got the message by nodding, agreeing with the completely unspoken statement you have made that you really have to part now!

If she does not give any of these signals, you will repeat the whole thing again. You will do it much more obviously – until finally, in desperation, you may be reduced to words: 'I really must be off...'

And then the last stages of the ritual, the actual farewell. There will almost always be a smile of acknowledgement, a head 'bow' of respect, and a slight forwards lean before you edge away. You will often touch the other person, in varying ways depending on the situation. Young people, men, acquaintances, business partners and those who have spent just a short time together will tend to touch less – perhaps just a pat on the arm or a handshake. Children, women, old friends and those who have just spent a long time together will tend to touch more – a full body hug, or a kiss. Culture too matters – British people are notoriously low on parting touches, while the French always shake hands, and Belgian women offer three kisses on alternating cheeks!

Then, you separate. Possibly you walk backwards for just a moment as you part, keeping each other in view as if in order to delay the parting. As the distance increases, you will start to use gestures and expressions better able to be seen from afar. You will smile more noticeably, raise your eyebrows, use some kind of wave – from the hardly noticeable finger salute through to the ultimate in enthusiasm – two waving arms held high above your head.

Goodbye!

4 ♥ Making Love Work

How Can Body Language Help Me Succeed in Love?

Love relationships, perhaps more than any other, rely on body language to succeed. Loving is such a physical thing, so dependent on bodies harmonizing as well as minds, that intimate partnership without an awareness of body language may never develop to its full potential.

In the early stages of a relationship, often you are both so wary of rejection that it is just too embarrassing to talk openly about what is happening – or rather, about what you hope might be happening. You need body language, then, to read your prospective partner's signals and to make sure that yours are clear and unambiguous. You both need an awareness of nonverbal communication also to make sure that you are setting the scene correctly, and moving things on at the right pace.

Next, your relationship will probably move into a phase where, in some ways, there is nothing but body language – where sex is the main thing on the agenda. Here a knowledge of each other's bodies and each other's sexual body language is crucial once again, this time to allow you to pleasure each other in the right way – or to tell when you are making love in a way that is not pleasurable.

As the partnership settles, you need an awareness of emotional signals to help you spot difficulties ahead of time. It is now known that body language can signal these difficulties long before you are consciously aware of them. And you can also both use body language to work through any problems, to minimize the damage by reacting positively to each other.

When you are in love, the whole future of your partnership can depend on signalling this love not only with your words but with everything you do.

What Can I Wear to Attract a Partner?

If you want to attract a partner, the first thing you have to do is to get her (or him) to notice you. So whether your initial move is being made in a disco or in a coffee bar, at evening class or at a party, dress to draw people's eyes towards you.

Remember, though, that different genders will notice different things. Women are more likely to be enthusiastic about fashion and are often more colour-aware; you can therefore get a woman's attention by making an informed fashion statement and by being colour-coordinated. Men, on the other hand, are generally physiologically excited quite simply by physical features, though they are often also stimulated by strong colours; therefore, you might try to get a man's attention by wearing figure-hugging clothes and bright, rich tones. (This gender difference can also, of course, create problems: a man wearing tight jeans may be seen by women as sexually 'too obvious'; a woman wearing the latest style may be wasting her money trying to impress a man in this way, as he will probably not even notice her fashion statement.)

Secondly, to attract a partner what you wear needs to reflect who you are. For clothes can make a number of statements about you. Outrageous outfits will suggest that you are a confident extrovert. Toned-down, classic styles will suggest that you are more cautious and traditional. Expensive outfits and Oxfam dressing will both seem to hint, in different ways, at your bank balance. Power suits (for either gender) or well-worn jeans will seem as if they are giving out certain information about your interests or your lifestyle.

Be careful, though. The statement you make with your clothes will only really work if, first, it is an accurate reflection of who you are and, secondly, if your prospective partner is attracted by that statement. If your clothes, hairstyle and jewellery are outrageous, then whether or not you are actually a screaming extrovert you will attract people who want an outrageous partner. If you dress in a down-market way, then you will attract someone who does not want her (or his) partner to be smart and affluent.

The final secret of dressing for relationship success is that, while most people fall in love with what they see, they stay in love with what they feel. So dress to encourage contact. Many clothes are off-putting because they look stiff, unyielding or too fragile to touch. A business suit can seem like a coat of armour; jangling jewellery can literally keep a partner at arm's length. Instead, when with your partner make her (or him) want to reach out and touch you by wearing smooth silk, soft bouclé, or crisp cotton.

Make your fashion decisions not only by eye but also by hand, always checking what you buy, as you buy it, for whether it feels good as well as looks good. If you do, then as your relationship develops your partner will continue to want to touch you as well as simply to be with you.

How Can I Tell Who Is Available and Who Is Not?

In Victorian society women wore their hair up to show they were married. In many Indian cultures women wear the sari only after their wedding. But in Western society the formal signals are much more mixed. Is a person available? The only really universal symbol we have, a ring on the third finger of the left hand, may nowadays simply be a ring, and not a symbol of marriage. And even if it is, it can easily be removed in the cause of short-term availability!

Much more accurate than these formal signals are the spontaneous ones that a body naturally sends out when a person wants to show that he (or she) is available to a potential partner.

He will begin by putting himself 'on display'. In physical terms, whatever his age or situation he will show the world just how healthy and fit he is. His muscle tone increases, any puffiness round his eyes disappears, his skin may look clearer. A slight increase in heart rate and blood-pressure brings colour to his cheeks and brightens his eyes. He will stand up straighter, move with more agility.

There will also be gender displays: Men square and broaden their shoulders, and pull in their stomachs and buttocks to create the classic masculine ideal. Women pull their shoulders back to display breasts, cross and stretch out legs to emphasize their length, angle themselves to show off hips and thighs. Both genders will also unconsciously 'preen' – making themselves look more attractive by patting their hair into place, licking their lips, straightening their clothes.

At the same time, someone who is available will also signal that he wants to make contact. The whole focus of his body language will be outwards, using completely open signals that angle out towards potential partners, facing directly outwards and smiling an unconscious, welcoming half-smile, regularly scanning the room or the group with his eyes. (A 'non-available' person, on the other hand, male or female, will tend to focus his or her posture and eye contact only towards the group he or she is with, while a person whose partner is present and who is committed to that partner will tend, even unconsciously, to aim body language mainly towards that partner.)

Will these signals always tell you accurately who is available and who is not? In general, yes – but beware. If someone is shy, lacking in self-confidence or inhibited, then whether or not he is available his shoulders will droop, his gaze will drop, and all his body language will say 'Ignore me ... go away.'

Also, often embarrassingly, availability signals can be sent loud and clear by someone already spoken for. A person's body will respond instinctively with all the signs mentioned here if he sees someone he would like to mate with – whether or not he is free to do so. The body language of availability only reflects what the person wants – not whether legally or morally he is in a position to take up on any offers!

What Makes a Good Flirt – and Should I Learn to Be One?

Flirting – the skill of encouraging a prospective partner – is a very ancient art indeed. Though spontaneous, it also has very definite stages; a good flirt masters and uses them all.

First, there is the 'come on', which lets the other person know that you are really interested. You will send out all the body language signals of attraction, but magnified, turning completely towards the other person, leaning forward so that you are nearly touching, maintaining prolonged eye contact. You will probably also, without even realizing it, also send out signals of advanced sexual arousal – your voice will drop several tones; your breathing will become more rapid; your skin may flush.

Once you are sure that the other person is responding, an accomplished flirt will use the 'pull-back'. This is a slight withdrawal of all these attraction signals, aimed to make your prospective partner feel just slightly insecure, to show her (or him) just what he will be missing if he does not take advantage of what you are offering. You may look away, look sideways, lower your eyelids, use your hand or a wine glass to mask your expression – in Spain, women use the fan for just this purpose.

Then, in case your partner starts 'pulling back', you add the 'block off', which turns the attention firmly on to you alone. You may shift so that your body actually shields your partner from other people; men often stretch out their legs as a block off, while women are more likely to use their hand movements to form a barrier to the world. You may slip your partner's name into what you are saying – as a person's name is the word most likely to catch her attention.

Lastly, once you have a prospective partner's full attention, you add the closing element of flirting: the 'promise' – an intimation of things to come. You may find an excuse to touch, by sharing a menu or passing a glass of wine. You may touch yourself, to remind your partner what it would be like to touch you and what it would be like to have you touch her (or him). So your hand may absentmindedly stroke your face, your tongue may lick your lips, you may run sensuous fingers through your hair.

Can you learn to be a flirt? The four steps sound straightforward, but they also need to be natural. So if you try any of the above when you are drunk, then you will simply look silly. If you try any of them too soon, before your prospective partner is really ready, this may be a turn-off. If you flirt in an exaggerated way – laughing uncontrollably rather than smiling enigmatically, for example – then the element of mystery at the heart of true flirting will be lost.

What you can do, however, is to become aware of your own natural flirting style and work with it. Some of the flirting patterns described here will come easily to you; others will seem contrived. Steer clear of the latter, and cultivate the former. Be aware of what you are doing, be aware of your partner's response – when she (or he) seems aroused and when turned off. Quite simply, do what works – and remember that with flirting, less always means more.

What Is the Best Way to Suggest a Date?

Why deal, in a book on body language, with a topic like making a date? Surely that is all to do with words? But body language can help you use those words more effectively – by understanding your prospective partner's nonverbal signals, and checking that your own are giving the right messages.

First, check nonverbally whether any offer of a further meeting will actually be welcomed. Is the other person showing interest – not necessarily the full-blown sexuality of a flirtatious come-on, but the friendly encouragement of looking and smiling? Do not worry too much if you pick up tension signals such as a nervous laugh or tense cough; your prospective partner is more likely to be worried that you will not get the chance to meet again than wary that you will.

One foolproof way to check whether the other person feels you are getting on well, and therefore whether he (or she) will probably welcome an invitation, is this: Are the two of you 'matching' – that is, unconsciously copying each other in some way? Are you taking up the same position, or shifting position within seconds of each other? Are your gestures synchronized? Are you laughing at the same time, in the same way? If so, then it is likely that you are both at one with each other.

How should you suggest a date? The words will be yours alone; but check that your body language is not undermining those words. Nervousness can mean that you sound and seem over-casual – your gaze moving up, down and everywhere but at the other person when making your suggestion, your voice tailing off at the end of the sentence. You may hesitate, stumble, or contradict yourself. Because he (or she) feels insecure, the other person may well interpret these signals to mean that you are wary of him – rather than wary of rejection. So be confident; take a deep breath, face him directly, look directly at him. And smile – which will not only make you look more welcoming but, by loosening your vocal chords, will make you sound more enthusiastic too.

On the other hand, nervousness could also make you sound over-pushy. A fear of rejection may make you take up a challenging position, shoulders squared as if for a fight, your gaze confrontational, your tone of voice loud and aggressive. No wonder your prospective partner backs off! Instead, lower your defences. Allow your shoulders to drop, your gaze to meet the other person's gently. Lower your tone of voice slightly as you speak – though make sure that the volume does not drop nervously away towards the end of each sentence.

As your prospective partner gives his answer, check his body language. A long pause, with his eyes sliding off to one side and his body slightly turned away, signals some doubts. If the other person's voice is hesitant and if his smile seems false because it does not quite reach his eyes, then he may be trying to let you down gently. But if he turns towards you with a full and genuine smile, and his body movements seem to speed up enthusiastically, then celebrate. Your offer has not only been accepted, it is also very obviously welcome.

How Can I Use Body Language to Make Sure that a First Date Goes Well?

One of the key foundations of a successful date is relaxation. If you both feel able to unwind with each other, then you will be far more likely to enjoy yourselves – and far more likely to get on well together. So do all you can, nonverbally, to be relaxed.

To begin with, get your timing right. Do not choose a time of day when you are likely to feel pressured, such as a lunch hour – unless, of course, you want an excuse to get away if things do not go well. And if you can, choose a time when you know you are at your best; if you are someone whose body demands sleep just after the nine o'clock news, then plan to meet early in the evening – or the nonverbal message you will send to your partner may be 'lack of interest'!

Equally, some settings are more relaxing than others. At the beginning of a relationship, meeting in a neutral venue such as a wine bar can feel safer than visiting each other's homes. Sharing an activity such as bowling or walking may feel less pressured than simply sitting talking one-to-one, and will also, by releasing your nervous adrenalin, physically relax you too.

The classic 'date activity' of going for a meal is also a tension reducer. First, most restaurants that are not simply selling fast food are specifically designed to de-stress you: their dim lighting and soft music creates a soporific effect, while the fact that you are being looked after (by the restaurant staff) allows you to 'let go' and not worry. Physiologically too, your body will actually relax while eating, with or without the addition of alcohol with the meal. It is difficult to feel insecure with someone you have shared a meal with.

Even after all this, however, you and your partner may feel tense or nervous. The way to reduce these feelings for both of you is actually to concentrate on your partner and signal nonverbally that she (or he) is interesting. Doing this will relax you because you will not feel you have to perform. And it will relax your partner because humans spontaneously unwind if they are given interest signals. Feeling your approval, your partner's muscle tension will fade away.

So use all the nonverbal cues you can which indicate interest and sympathy. Keep your eyes on your partner, rather than just staring into space when she speaks. Respond with a slight nod of your head whenever you agree with or like what your partner is saying. Allow your emotions to parallel your partner's, so that if she talks about something that concerns her, you look concerned, and if she is delighted, you smile too.

Knowing that you are interested in her, your partner will start to show her interest in you – and in time, both of you will increasingly feel positive about each other. What more could you want of a date?

How Can I Arrange My Personal Space to Facilitate Romance?

When a date is over and you go back home together, the setting can make romance a possibility – or an improbability. The key is that anything that moves you both slowly and safely towards sensing and feeling will help. But anything that gets you thinking – particularly about everyday realities or insecurities – will hinder, by making it less likely that you will be able simply to feel.

To begin with then, here are some Don'ts: Don't open the door to a room cluttered with dirty dishes, rubbish, shopping lists or other things associated with daily living; they will distract your partner as well as you. Don't leave the phone on the hook or the answer-phone turned to full volume; you will both listen to the message when it comes through. And don't make a clear statement of intent, such as black satin sheets or condoms out in full view; you may both get anxious if forced to think about sex too early and in too direct a way.

Instead, aim for sensuality. The classic romantic 'scene-setting' of soft lights, soft music and a soft sofa is, in nonverbal terms, very effective. For by reducing what you see and hear, you will be able to concentrate on what you feel.

So dim the lighting a little, but not too much; darkness with soft pools of light works best. Soft, womb-like lighting has been shown to encourage soft-focus gazing, soft talking and increased touching – though too dim a room can simply make you fall asleep, or feel threatened by too much darkness and so tense up.

Lower the volume, opting for instrumental music with a low, slow tone and a deep rhythmic beat – a combination that not only increases safety (by reminding you of that most reassuring of sounds, the human heartbeat) but also makes you more likely to want physical contact.

Then, to make that contact easier, make sure there is somewhere you can sit together. Again, make sure it feels safe. Avoid squashing up against each other so that you both feel invaded or threatened – and avoid sitting on a bed that is so obviously a bed that you feel you are expected to leap into it. The ideal is a comfortable sofa with soft cushions, and with no plants, bolsters, lamps or occasional tables to get in the way when you want to move closer together.

Finally, fill your environment with ways to make that move, particularly if you are not yet intimate and need excuses to be close. A bottle of wine or a bubbling coffee percolator mean that you have to alter your position in order to pour for each other. An interesting book or photo album creates a reason to sit closer as you look at it together. A cat, demanding attention, can easily be stroked by both of you. Given such reasons for making contact, it will be very easy to find yourselves spontaneously touching...

How Can I Make the 'First Move' Effectively?

When we say 'first move' – meaning the initial intimate touch or kiss – we are not actually talking about a 'first' move at all. Making contact with someone sexually is a step many stages along the road of a relationship. Before it happens, lots of other physical moves should have been made – and if you are not aware of that, then you may act too soon and ruin everything.

When you and a prospective partner get together, you go through a long and unconscious procedure of checking each other out nonverbally. You look, you listen, you move just slightly closer – all this above and beyond the words. Then, when you are sure you want to take things further, you begin with unthreatening, nonsexual contact – 'excuse' touches that can always be ignored if one of you panics and backs off. You sit close enough for your arms to touch; you pass a menu and brush hands; you accidentally rub shoulders at the table. This contact is made, very briefly, by one of you. The other subconsciously notices it and decides whether it feels right or not. And if it does not feel right, then nothing more happens.

If it does feel right, then it is the other person's turn to find an excuse and touch. If your partner has patted your arm to emphasize a point, then a few minutes later you may give him (or her) a playful dig in the ribs. These touches may not seem like a lead-up to sex – and that is the whole point. They are a way of checking out the possibilities long before sex is clearly on the agenda, so that neither of you moves too quickly, or without being welcomed.

So touches develop, are offered, accepted and then returned. And slowly the touches become more obvious, more lingering, more risky – grasping a companion's hand when crossing the road, linking arms when walking along the street. And you both naturally get ready for the step into that more obvious 'move', such as a kiss, which will make it absolutely clear you are both attracted to each other in a sexual way.

The secret to making that more obvious move effectively is to make sure that both of you have already made all the previous moves. You cannot afford to leap in if a stage has been missed. So if you attempt a kiss without the earlier stages of contact, then your partner may feel rushed and pull back. And if you have created several opportunities to touch him, but those touches simply have not been returned, then however friendly your companion seems he simply is not ready or willing to move on to a sexual relationship with you.

At the same time, are you moving too slowly? If your partner has offered a touch, and you have not returned it – possibly because you feel that you have imagined it – then you may be giving the impression that you are not interested. So be aware of what is happening and respond. Remember that becoming intimate is not something you do on your own. Both of you are involved; and both of you have to make a move if you are going to go any further.

How Can I Repel Advances I Do Not Want?

Whether you are a woman or a man, you may have to repel advances. We are not talking here about sexual harassment, but about the times in everyone's life when communication lines have become crossed. Someone thinks you want an intimate relationship, and she (or he) is wrong.

The first secret is to avoid situations where all the nonverbal messages seem to spell 'sex'. On page 130 there are guidelines on how to set the scene for romance; to avoid this, simply reverse the guidelines: Set the scene for talking rather than touching by choosing to sit in the kitchen rather than the living room, by turning the lights up high, by choosing light, loud music with lyrics.

Then protect yourself further by your specific body language. Make sure that your nonverbal messages are not sexual, such as deep prolonged eye contact or a soft husky tone of voice. Look away regularly, and keep your voice light and casual. In particular, make sure that you are not, even unconsciously, moving closer; literally keep your distance, at least the 1.2 m (4 ft) that keeps things firmly 'social' rather than 'personal'. Do not touch the other person, even accidentally, in case she thinks you are testing the ground for more sensual contact. If she touches you, stiffen noticeably, shift away slightly, stop interacting. If you do this regularly, every time a touch occurs, then without quite knowing consciously why, most people will stop trying to go further.

What if despite all this you do reach a point where you have to use the word 'no' because body language alone is not working? If so, make sure your nonverbal approach is not undermining what you are saying. This is particularly likely to happen if the person you are trying to fend off is a friend and you do not want to spoil the friendship. As a result, you may reach out, smile reassuringly, use a soft tone of voice. Your companion may then confuse these signals with those of encouragement.

Instead, make sure that your body language gives the same message as your words. Do not touch. Look serious, speak clearly. There is no need to be hostile, but there is every need to be direct and unambiguous. That way you can halt the problem and move your relationship back to the comfortable but nonsexual friendship that you really want.

Is There a Secret to Perfect Kissing?

Kissing is one of the most intimate ways of showing love. It is powerful not only because it creates passion, not only because it allows us to exchange body chemicals which make us feel closer to each other. According to some experts, kissing is also powerful because it takes us back to deeply-buried historical memories of the safety and affection of infancy – because kissing originally developed from mothers weaning their babies with chewed-up food passed from mouth to mouth.

There are hundreds of different types of kisses – different in the way you move, the speed, the firmness, different in the way you use your lips, your tongue and even your teeth! And really, the only secret to perfect kissing is, quite simply, to be aware of all the possibilities, and then to allow yourselves to respond naturally to what each of you wants.

Remember first all the different ways there are to begin a kiss. The classic, seen in the movies, is when you lock eye contact and move slowly together. But then there is the energetic and excited hug that somehow makes mouths as well as bodies collide. There is the soft warm cuddle where one mouth reaches down and the other up. There is the 'single-sider' where one partner gently nuzzles his (or her) way from ear to mouth while the other lies back and enjoys it.

As lips meet, begin to explore the different ways to move and touch. Most kisses tend to work up gradually to a peak of arousal. So you may want to begin with less passionate kisses – slow, gentle, dry with lips closed or just parted. As passion builds, so the kisses can begin to speed up and firm up, with your bodies moving along with the kiss. You may start to nibble, bite playfully, vary the pressure of lips, vary the rhythm and speed. The secret here is to make a move, check your partner's body signals and then respond, either moving forward or pulling back.

As passion builds, so your lips will part. Maybe your tongues will meet, and kisses will become more moist. This not only arouses you – the sebaceous glands at the corner of your lips and within your mouth send out semio-chemical signals that stimulate you. Tongue-kisses also give you extra, valuable experience about one another, because by paralleling the sex act they allow each of you to learn a little more about how the other responds intimately.

End your kiss in the way that feels perfect to you. Does letting your mouths part slowly mean that you turn the kiss into a passionate hug? Does ending the clinch with several brief, light kisses mean that you separate lovingly? Or will you choose to pull away firmly, as if to end the embrace there – and then just smile and start kissing all over again?

Are There Any Guaranteed Ways to Turn My Partner On?

The answer to this question is no. Everyone has different sexual tastes. This is not only because we come from different cultures where different things are seen as erotic – in some Eastern cultures, for example, 'love biting' is an advanced art. It is not only because we come from different genders – men are more instantly excited by what they see, while women are more aroused by what they hear. But also, we are different because our previous sexual experiences have given us different preferences.

So you have to be prepared to start afresh with each new partner, learning about her (or his) body, learning what turns her on, unlearning what you think turns her on but in fact does not.

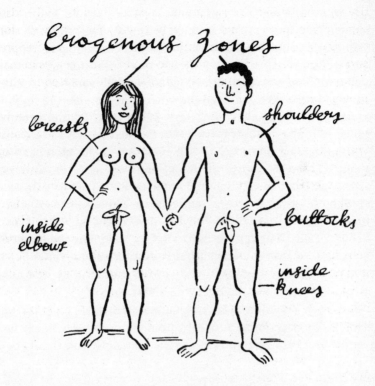

Erogenous Zones

breasts

shoulders

inside elbows

buttocks

inside knees

Find out, to start with, which parts of your partner's body are the most sensitive. The term 'erogenous zone' has been used to describe the more usual sensitive areas. Both men and women will usually enjoy touch on the face, shoulders, hands, buttocks and genitals. A man will also particularly enjoy stimulation at the base of his spine – which, sensitively done, can bring him to erection – and a woman will often find touch wonderful on her breasts, the back of her neck, and the insides of her elbows and knees. But tastes vary: many men love having their nipples touched, while some women hate it. And body areas that leave some partners cold can drive others wild.

Having discovered your partner's particular erogenous zones, then explore just how to arouse. Touch is the basic way – but there are many different sorts of touch. You can stroke, rub, tickle, scratch, pat, massage – even pinch or smack. You can touch with fingers and palms – but also with your face, toes, tongue, nipples, long sensuous hair, a penis, a clitoris, or even ostrich feathers and a vibrator. You can touch firmly, lightly, or with variation. You can go slow, fast, or first one then the other. You can alter the rhythm, or slow to a complete stop and keep your partner waiting, stretched to the limit of pleasure, for the next touch.

Above and beyond all this, the biggest turn-on for most people is mood. So become aware of the different moods that turn your partner on – and what you can do nonverbally to recreate those by blending setting, 'props' and sexual body language. Does romance arouse – and if so, is that soft lights, dim music, a fur rug or candlelight? Does your partner like to fight a bit among the cushions, or make love against a wall? Does your partner sometimes like to be totally nurtured, cradled, perhaps fed mouthful by mouthful, then undressed slowly before being pleasured?

The truth is that there are no guarantees in sex – only trial and error. So try everything, and learn from your mistakes. It may take a while to get things right – but in the meantime you should both have a lot of fun!

What Body Language Should I Use When My Partner and I Undress?

If your partnership is a new one, then undressing may be a nerve-wracking event. If your partnership is well-established, then it may be a non-event. In both cases, body language can help.

The first time you undress can be a risky occasion for a number of reasons. Both of you may fear that when clothes come off, your partner will be unimpressed by what is revealed. A 1994 British survey suggested that the vast majority of women, of whatever size, are concerned that they are overweight; particular fears are that of a bulging tummy or thighs. Equally, many women are worried about the shape of their breasts – anxious that they are too small, too large, too floppy. Men, on the other hand, tend to worry most about the size of their penis and whether they have a firm erection.

For all these reasons it is important to make undressing in front of each other for the first time a positive experience. Set the scene, with a well-heated room and flatteringly dim lights; make sure you will not be disturbed by the telephone, pets, flatmates or children. It is wise to avoid undressing in separate rooms, as that makes the moment of revelation all the more stressful. Equally, do not strip in turn, as that means that all eyes are on the 'performer'. Instead, you may want to begin playfully, with jokes, giggles and some rough and tumble; laughter is a physical stress-releaser and will prevent tension rising, particularly if a hook gets caught or a zipper stuck.

When your relationship is well established, the problems are different. The risk of undressing is almost too low, so it is no longer an exciting experience. You may be used to seeing each other in the nude, and your body language when naked is now casual, matter-of-fact and not in the least seductive.

Once again, set the scene, with all the romantic icons of candle-light and music. Once again, make sure you will not be disturbed. But then, experiment with different, more risky ways of undressing. Strip in turn, making a show for each other, maybe even to music. Take off everything but one piece of clothing and make love in that. Play strip poker (or tiddlywinks, or any game where you can each win in turn) with the loser giving the usual forfeit. Or alternate playing a passive role: you lie still while your partner undresses you and then pleasures you – without you moving a muscle.

Alternatively, you may want to make the occasion an opportunity to rediscover romance, with dimmed lights and slow seductive disrobing, piece by piece interspersed with passion. As you undress, show your appreciation of each other constantly, by look-ing, kissing, touching – one experienced lover suggests that from the moment you start undressing, you should aim never to lose physical contact with each other completely.

The key is this: If you can set the scene for passion before you start to undress, then you will have a much better chance of being passionate once you have left your clothes behind.

How Can I Tell How Aroused My Partner Is?

Human beings send out two kinds of nonverbal signs to show we are aroused. The most basic are those uncontrollable physiological signs that the body naturally produces. The other are what you might call 'codes', body language signals that we learn over time as we get more sexually experienced.

The uncontrollable signals are the body's unconscious way of signalling passion. A good lover notes them the first time he (or she) makes love with a new partner, and explores them further as the relationship develops, to sense the pace at which lovemaking is moving and to adapt his technique accordingly.

So if you want to become an expert on your partner's arousal, first, listen. You may hear his breathing rate increase regularly and steadily; his heart rate increases, his tone of voice drops and becomes husky. Also look; you may see a flushing or slight swelling as blood flows into areas that get more sensitive during sex – not only the penis (or clitoris), but the lips, nipples, ears and buttocks. Be aware too of a change in skin texture, as muscle tone changes with the physiological preparation for the sex act. And notice moisture – all body fluids such as saliva, sweat and vaginal (or penile) secretions will increase with arousal.

But also be aware of the other type of nonverbal signals of arousal, the ones we use consciously. These codes of movement and sound vary from person to person. As a partner feels more aroused, he (or she) may move faster, harder and more urgently, start to sob and cry with pleasure – or may become very still and silent, as if to concentrate on the sensations he feels. Your partner may use particular sounds and words to mean 'more, more' – or develop light touches and gestures to show you just what he wants you to do.

Using these 'codes' can be amazingly useful. If your partner learns to signal with a particular kind of moan that a particular touch is wonderful, and if you learn to respond to that, then over time you will be able to please each other more and more. Rather than learning how to make love by the book, you will quite simply learn to do more of what works, and less of what doesn't. It is a recipe for ecstasy.

How Can My Partner and I Best Learn from Each Other in Bed?

Telling each other what you like in bed is always good. But the key way to learn is to show, rather than tell. If you can demonstrate what you like, each of you pleasuring yourself so that the other can see just what to do and just how to do it, then you can learn more in an hour than in several nights of pillowtalk.

You may feel uncertain; masturbating in front of someone else is never easy. So set the scene, making sure you are comfortable –

and won't be interrupted. Take it in turns, first to find the precise position that suits you – while one person may want to sit up against cushions, another may prefer to lie down. And instruct your partner exactly how you want her (or him) to participate, perhaps holding you, perhaps not touching you at all.

When you are the observer, watch closely. Learn just how your partner gets just the sensations she or he likes, and in what way. How does your partner touch herself – using hands, pressing thighs together, rubbing up against cushions, using a vibrator? Where does she touch: on the tip of the clitoris, with the clitoral hood pulled back … on the penis, with hand wrapped round, foreskin pulled back … with a finger also inserted into the anus or the mouth? What type of movement does your partner use – fast or slow, hard or soft, rhythmic or spasmodic? And if your partner comes to a climax, what tips her over the top; does the movement need to change, the rhythm alter, the pressure increase?

You may want to masturbate in front of each other more than once to learn what really works. Also, you may want to include this as a regular part of lovemaking. But you can also put into practice with each other all you have learned from watching when you masturbate each other. Can you use the same positions that you liked when you were masturbating? Can you cuddle your partner in just the way she (or he) likes to be held? Can you touch in all the right places; with fingers, tongue, vibrator; with the right type of movement; with the right variation of speed and rhythm? Can you use all that you have learned to bring your partner to a climax in just the way she or he has always wanted?

Then, use your added technique to enhance intercourse. For while some of the things that work when you pleasure yourself do not work when someone else does them, many of them will give added value to penetrative sex. Try using each other's masturbation rhythms during penetrative lovemaking. Try adapting the positions you like when self-pleasuring, so that at least one of you is enjoying penetration that way. In particular, try stimulating your female partner's clitoris during intercourse in the way she does when she masturbates; this can actually mean the difference between her reaching orgasm – or not.

When Is the Time Right for Penetration?

Now or later? When a couple make love, when exactly should penetration happen to make sure that both partners get the most pleasure?

For a man, things are fairly obvious and straightforward. When he has a strong and confident erection, he can certainly penetrate – even if he does choose to wait a while to excite himself even further. If he does not have an erection, penetration can actually create one; if his partner sits on top or in a position where the penis can be guided in gently, or takes his penis into the mouth, wonderful things can happen!

For a woman, though, it is not nearly so easy to tell when the time is right; she does not have that one obvious sign of readiness, clear for all to read. The answer is for both partners to learn more about the woman's arousal pattern. Then when she feels prepared, she can say so in words or with body language – and her partner can be sure of when she is ready.

When a woman becomes aroused, her genitals go through several changes. Her uterus expands and lifts, her vagina begins to open and widen, her outer and inner genital lips part and become filled with blood to increase their sensitivity. Her vagina becomes filled with fluid, and then may contract. Her clitoris may harden and become erect – just as a penis does.

As a woman, you may actually feel all this happening as you get more excited. Be aware of your vagina starting to feel 'empty'; feel it starting to throb and palpitate. You may feel a final rush of moisture and a warmth as blood rushes into the genital area. You may feel other parts of your body, such as your nipples and buttocks, become suddenly very sensitive. It is at this point that you may want to signal to your partner that the time is right for penetrative sex, perhaps by letting your thighs open, by touching your partner in a way that draws you together – or by any of the other ways that you have developed between you of signalling your readiness.

A woman's partner can also sense her inner changes, particularly if willing to explore and chart her differing responses as she gets more aroused. Her vagina may flood with moisture – though beware, this alone is not an accurate signal; she may not yet be sufficiently aroused for penetration to be comfortable. If you are touching her genitals with your fingers, however, you may actually feel her vagina open – and then pull at your finger as it contracts. If you are licking her genitals, you may sense a subtle shift in odour as she becomes fully aroused.

If you are aware of all these signals, and use your body language skills to read them and interpret them, then you will both have a good chance of avoiding too early a move. You will make sure that penetration is always the pleasure that it should be.

How Can I Tell When My Partner Has Climaxed?

An orgasm is the peak of sexual pleasure. The longest ever recorded lasted for 43 seconds and, like all orgasms, involved muscle spasms throughout the pelvis, a dramatic increase in heart rate, breathing and blood-pressure, and a contented relaxation afterwards. It was probably fairly obvious when that climax happened!

It is also usually fairly obvious when a man has his climax because he ejaculates. First, there is a rush of blood up the penis and a minute spurt of pre-ejaculate. Then, the pelvic muscles contract and semen shoots from the penis, spurting every eight-tenths of a second. Afterwards, the man's erection will probably dip, at least for a while. If his penis was in his partner's vagina at the time of climax, then she will probably have experienced a sudden hardness, increased moisture, then a shrinking of the penis away from the walls of her vagina.

Fascinatingly, however, all of the above is not always true. Men can have an orgasm without ejaculating – the art of doing so is part of Tantric sexuality. It is one way of practising family planning – though if you are tempted to try it, remember that it takes many years of training and, in that time, many babies can be inadvertantly made!

What happens for a woman when she climaxes is a mirror image of what happens for a man. The muscles near the base of the spine and the rectum contract, again at intervals of eight-tenths of a second, creating ripples of pleasure which may involve the vagina, rectum and clitoris. Her climax may involve a stiffening of limbs, a total slackening of muscles, cries of pleasure – or simply a sigh of contentment.

The problem is, of course, that whereas a man's climax (i.e., ejaculation) is obvious, a woman's is not. So is there a way you can tell if your partner has had her orgasm?

Vaginal contractions are hard to fake – only a woman with great pelvic control can do so. And all the climax signals that are sent out by the nervous system are usually unfakable. So listen for a slow but regular increase in the rhythm of your partner's breathing. Notice a sharp rise in heart rate. Look for a red flush across her chest and breasts. And be aware of the pulling of the vaginal muscles against your finger or penis.

If you do not observe these signs, do not panic. It does not mean that your partner has not climaxed. Maybe her orgasm was too gentle for these signals to show. But if you do see them, then you can be almost certain that your partner has reached her orgasm – and that is a cause of celebration for you both.

What Are the Body Language 'Contraceptives' I Can Use If I Do Not Want to Make Love?

In every long-term relationship there are times when sex is not what you want. You do not feel bad about your partner, but you are tired or stressed. But often it is difficult to say so. Instead, you may unconsciously use body language, not only to indicate that you do not want to be intimate, but also actually to turn your partner off and make it less likely that you will make love. How do you do this?

Your initial strategy will be to use signals that are the direct opposite of all the ones you normally use to attract your partner. Instead of standing tall, showing off your best points, flirting or looking passionate, you will slump, slow down your movements, curl in on yourself as if hiding your best features. Your body may spontaneously lose muscle tone, your skin may look slightly faded, your face become slack and round; you do not look sexually attractive because, without realizing it you do not want to be sexually attractive.

At the same time you may start putting up body language barriers with crossed arms and legs. You may turn away if your partner approaches, and busy yourself with whatever else you are doing. You may even, without realizing it, start using hostile body language in order to keep your partner at bay. You may not, of course, actually feel at all irritable or aggressive, but if you wish to avoid making love for any reason, you may frown slightly, lower your brows as if angry, start moving quickly, making a lot of noise or dropping things.

Or, you try a different strategy. While the body language of irritation can reduce a partner's sexual feelings by replacing them by antagonism, the body language of dependency can reduce sexual feelings by replacing them with a desire to nurture. So you may take on a childlike expression, use a babyish tone of voice. You may cling on to your partner wearily, as if in need of support – building on your first unconscious strategy of looking tired and faded. In response, your partner may start to feel protective rather than passionate; all sexual desire dies away, to be replaced by a desire to look after you.

You may end up in bed – but it will be with a hot water bottle and an aspirin rather than with a hot partner and a condom!

How Can I Tell What My Partner Is Really Feeling?

Whatever kind of relationship you have with your partner, being able to read and respond to his (or her) emotions will deepen that relationship. Particularly, noticing if your partner is anxious, irritated or sad will help you support him when you need to.

When someone feels an emotion, his body alerts him to some event that is actually happening, or some thought that he is thinking, and prepares him for action. Originally, this 'alert and preparation' was the body's way of gearing up physiologically for such essential actions as fighting an opposing tribe or running away from a bear. Nowadays, of course, people react with strong emotion to such modern essentials as a looming job interview or the news that their car has been stolen!

A physiological response like this almost always reveals itself in signals on the outside of the body. And even though today, humans are actually encouraged to hide such signals and seem unemotional for much of the time, subtle signs will be there for you to see.

An anxious or worried partner, for example, is protecting himself from something that scares him. He will raise his eyebrows and draw them together as if for protection, frowning in a way that among apes means that they are trying to escape from something but cannot. Your partner may look slightly bowed, his shoulders and head down, almost as if defending himself from attack. He may use 'escape' movements – little wriggles of his fingers or toes.

A sad partner, on the other hand, is one who has suffered a loss or a disappointment. He will signal this in much the same way as young primates signal their need to be looked after. He will sit still or move without energy. His mouth will turn down at the corners, his voice will be low and slow. Even if he does not weep, his eyelids may redden as the blood rushes there in preparation for tears, or a gleam of moisture may appear along his lower eyelids.

An irritated partner is one who, were human social rules against fighting not so strong, would fight. So his body language is that of combat. His eyes will stare, as if staring down the opposition; his eyebrows will be lowered and drawn together in an expression apes assume when ready to fight; his lips will be pushed forward as if in a snarl. Any sharp, urgent movements of his fingers and feet are here not 'escape' but 'engage' movements, as if he wants to hit out but cannot. His voice may be louder than normal, as it would be if he were trying to scare away an opponent.

Once you have recognized these emotional signs, then how you respond will depend on your partner, the situation and how you feel about how he feels. But often just acknowledging emotions can make a person feel better – and that guarantees a good basis for offering any kind of support your partner may need.

How Can I Tell What My Feelings Really Are About My Partner?

When something important happens in your relationship, your entire nervous system responds. Your heart rate increases, your blood-pressure soars, adrenalin pumps into your bloodstream, your digestion slows, your temperature peaks and your breathing speeds up. However briefly, your body gives you a 'jump start'. And this jump start creates all kinds of sensations within your body – so you might feel jumpy, twitchy, energetic, alert.

The fact that human beings feel emotions as internal sensations is acknowledged in our language, when we talk about 'butterflies in the stomach…a rush of anger…my stomach churned with fear…a broken heart…' These sensations of emotion have a very real purpose; they tell us when something is important, when we need to pay attention to it, when we need to do something about it.

Every person has her (or his) own particular set of emotional signals, depending on physiology, and also on how much the culture she lives in encourages her to be aware of emotions. Men in western society, for example, may ignore the internal signals of fear, because they are taught that fear is not manly. Women, on the other hand, may be encouraged to ignore internal signals of

anger. But you can begin to be familiar with your particular set of signals simply by allowing yourself to become aware of them as they happen.

Start by becoming aware of how you feel in general when you think about your partner. If your body starts seeming heavy, dragged down and sleepy, then this might indicate some sort of boredom or depression. If there is a warm prickliness around your eyes and a tight feeling in your throat, then you may want to shed tears over some aspect of the relationship. If you feel energetic and alert, then the relationship is one that is stimulating you and making you happy.

Concentrate particularly on signals in the area of your body that surrounds your spine. It is down your spine that your nerves transmit signals to and from your brain and the rest of your body; and so it is in the parts of your body that are near the spine – stomach, gut, chest or back muscles – that you may expect to feel the signals your body sends you when it registers a strong emotion. So, for example, if you feel excited about meeting up with your partner you may get a rising, bubbly feeling in your gut. If you are irritated by your partner's words you may feel yourself flushing bright red across your chest. If you are anxious about the relationship you may get a churning in your stomach.

Note the feeling, whether it is pleasant or unpleasant. Notice if it brings any thoughts to your mind. For even if you are not sure what some sudden back tension really says about your relationship, you will probably infer that your body is under some kind of stress. And even if you do not know why you are suddenly more relaxed when with your partner, you will probably realize that it indicates some change for the better.

Becoming aware of these signals and starting to work out what they mean can give you a new way to start understanding your feelings – and a new way to start improving your relationship.

How Can I Spot Relationship Problems Before They Start?

Some signals of relationship problems are very obvious. Are you acting in a hostile way? Raised voices, sour expressions or sad eyes reveal that you are angry, disillusioned or unhappy with each other. But well before these clear signs start to show, your body language may have already begun to signal problems more subtly.

Because imitation is the sincerest form of flattery, loving couples spontaneously 'match' each other's body language, copying posture, gestures, facial expressions or tones of voice.

So if you notice that you are no longer doing this, look carefully at what is happening between you. Did you once walk in step, and now mismatch pace? Did you once laugh in total synchrony – and now find that when one of you is deadly serious, the other is giggling? If so, then there is a nonverbal distance between you that was not there before.

This can show particularly in the way you anticipate each other's moves. Long-term partners know each other so well that they pick up the slightest cues – which direction the other is going to move in, or what gesture they are going to make next. If once you used to be able to move round each other in your tiny kitchen without effort, and now you are constantly bumping into each other, then you have lost awareness of each other's body language patterns.

You may notice that you are touching less. Many couples do relate with minimal touch, but if the level drops even further you need to worry. And if one or both of you is using blocking tactics – arms across the chest, or choosing to sit in chairs with arms that act as barriers – then you may be trying to avoid physical contact.

You may also no longer want to be emotionally close – and so you may be using body language designed to avoid communication. You may make your facial expression blank and your tone of voice carefully neutral, so that you simply do not reveal what you feel. And you may find yourselves no longer noticing each other's emotional signals; where once just the sound of your partner's voice when he (or she) came home from work told you what sort of day he'd had, now you may have to ask.

All these signals are merely the tip of the iceberg. Noticing them does not solve the problem; you will need to explore much more fully before you find out what the problem really is. What these signals do is alert you to difficulties, and so make it more likely that you will eventually be able to solve them.

How Can I Use Body Language to Turn an Argument into Something Useful?

Whether or not it is good for partners to get angry with each other in the first place is a question many psychologists have debated. But most couples do have rows. When they happen, once they have started and you are already angry, what do you do?

Here is how to use body language to turn a relationship sour: When you and your partner get angry with each other, try to ignore it. Refuse to talk; blank out all expression; avoid eye contact; become tightlipped; use a disapproving tone of voice. If all else fails, make the ultimate nonverbal statement – walk out. What this body language does is to stop you both handling your anger, or expressing it in a useful way. It is a bit like turning to each other when you are on the point of orgasm and telling yourselves to restrain the passion and stay calm.

For anger, like sex, stirs up all kinds of physical energy. If you have already begun to get angry, you have already begun to feel this energy inside and to express it in your body language outside. If instead you can channel it, then you can actually use this energy as a positive thing, and through that positive energy start to feel better about each other.

So instead of ignoring the anger, face it. Feel it inside you; become aware of just what the sensations are and how they are increasing. Then express yourselves with energy. Let your voices rise and be emphatic. Let your gestures be strong and large. Let your facial expressions reveal just what you feel. Never allow violence, of course; argue on opposite sides of a large room if you have to. But at the same time, never lose touch with each other – do not lose eye contact, do not refuse to talk, do not walk out.

If you do this and if you keep doing this, together, then within a short time you will find something strange happening. You will release the angry energy in your bodies and you will start to feel better. Maybe you will just both run out of words. Maybe you will both burst into laughter. Or maybe you will end up in bed – many couples do.

But whatever happens, you will have done something with the anger and not just pushed it under the carpet to fester.

And, that out of the way, you will then be able to talk about the issues calmly and sensibly. Though in fact, the chances are that afterwards neither of you will remember what on earth you were irritated about in the first place!

How Can I Really Tell If My Partner Is Having an Affair?

It is actually possible to hide misdemeanours from a partner for decades. If your partner starts an affair that lets her (or him) run her life in the same old way, you may never know there is a problem. If all the nonverbal patterns stay the same – such as the time she returns from work, or the number of times a week the two of you make love – you may never suspect a thing. It is only when the affair makes a difference in the way your partner behaves that you have any chance of guessing the truth.

So check timing: Is your partner suddenly available at different or unusual times, and unavailable at times when previously she was with you? Check location: A partner who suddenly avoids particular restaurants or pubs may be doing so because these are places she visits with her other lover.

Personal grooming is often a key: A woman who starts manicuring her nails or a man who starts using aftershave may be doing so for a lover. A partner who 'tastes' different when you kiss her may

actually have a new 'odour signature' as a result of having sex more often or with someone different.

Interestingly, these differences may not always seem negative. In fact some of them, at least in the short term, may seem like improvements. A partner who has a new lover may because of this develop an increased sex drive – and so may want sex more often with you. Or she may suddenly start making love in a new and interesting way.

Perhaps the easiest way to spot an affair is if you get a chance to see your partner together with her possible lover. If your suspicions are correct, you will almost surely notice a certain pattern to their behaviour towards each other. But these signs may not be the overt flirting that you might think; the kind of giggly, touchy behaviour that raises your hackles usually only happens between two people who are thinking of having an affair. If the affair has actually start-ed and there is something to hide, then your partner and her lover may actually be trying to control their conscious signs of passion.

So they may spend less time together, smile less, touch less, and pay each other less attention – in case you get suspicious.

On the other hand, they will still display unconscious signs that they are getting on better than ever before. So watch out for uncontrollable body language: 'display' signals of wide eyes, flushed skin or self-preening gestures; using hands and feet to 'point' to the object of attraction; copying or 'matching' each other's gestures, movements, tone of voice. All these signals are your partner's message to her lover that they are a couple – and her body language's message to you that you have something to worry about.

What Is the Best Body Language to Use When Breaking Bad News to My Partner?

Breaking bad news is always hard to do. Although using the right body language can never actually make bad news better, it can make a difference to the way your partner feels about the news you bring.

Start by considering when and where to break the news. What is the best time of day – first thing in the morning so that your partner has enough energy to cope with the stress he (or she) may feel, or at the end of the day when he has time to take in what has happened and deal with it? Where is the best setting? Most people can release emotions most safely at home, and shut off emotions when in public – which way of coping with feelings will be best for your partner? Being outdoors may allow you both to move about, which helps reduce feelings of stress – but if you suspect your partner will react very badly and perhaps be embarrassed about doing so in public, then you may choose to break the news in a private place.

Next, think about your own feelings. If you are anxious as you start talking to your partner, your posture may be tense, your gestures unsure, your voice shaky or stuttery. If you are angry about what you are saying, you may frown, speak sharply, use strong and aggressive gestures. The problem with all these signals is that – because recognizing, interpreting and also copying each other's body language is a key sign of partnership – your partner may not only sense problems from your nonverbal cues; he may also copy those cues and therefore feel just as anxious or irritated as you do, right from the start.

It is a good idea, then, to prepare by consciously relaxing and calming yourself down. Just before you meet your partner, stretch out, breathe deeply, deliberately try to ease your body tension. As you break the news, do your best to keep your body relaxed, your expression concerned, your voice low and calm.

How can you support your partner afterwards? If his first reaction is fury, he needs the freedom to move around in order to burn off the adrenalin that is flooding his body; stand clear and simply watch and listen. Otherwise, offer touch, which for most humans is comforting because it reminds them of being held when they were very young. Hold your partner's hand, sit side by side with your bodies touching, give him a hug. If your partner always feels stressed in a particular place on his body – a churning stomach, a tense back – then particularly offer touch there, with a supportive hand.

Once your partner has calmed down, you will both want to talk about what has happened. So use supportive body language as you listen: sit close to your partner; look at him; respond to his emotions with a nod, or a squeeze of the hand. Show him by every part of your body language that you want to help, and that all your partner has to do is ask.

What Happens to My Body – Outside and In – as I Move through the Various Stages of My Relationship?

Most love relationships follow a three-stage pattern. Human bodies have a sneaky physiological way of leading us inexorably on from one stage to the other – presumably so that, in the end, we will do what all human bodies are programmed to do from the start

– make babies. There is a first, desperate stage, when we are 'in love', or at any rate in lust. There is a second stage, when the initial euphoria has worn off and we start exploring whether we want to stay together. And, if we do, then there is a third stage where we make a commitment – to live together, get engaged, marry, settle down – and, with luck, see that commitment through.

So at the start, when you are just beginning a relationship, your body wants to keep you 'hooked' into it. If you are strongly attracted to someone, your brain produces a special chemical, the 'love drug' phenylethemine. Similar to substances found in chocolate and roses, this chemical keeps you on a high when you are with your partner, and makes you feel bad if you are apart. Like any other drug, it alters your physiological responses; you often cannot sleep, do not eat, lose weight. In body language terms, your aim is to show your love to your partner – you both use all the signals of attraction: gazing into each other's eyes, touching constantly, talking in a special, soft voice that you use for each other alone.

If all goes well, you move into the second phase. Your brain produces enkephalin, which increases your ability to see the best in things and makes you better able to bear pain – all of which helps you stay with your partner long enough to find out whether you are both suited. You calm down; your sleeping and eating patterns go back to normal. You still get on well with your partner. You may match each other in all sorts of obvious ways, such as eating the same sort of food and playing the same sort of music. But you are also more likely to disagree, and argue – because you are finding out what the differences are between you, and whether in the long term you can live with them. If you cannot, then you separate.

If you stay together, you enter the third stage of love. Your brain now produces endorphins, which make you feel secure and contented, which motivate you to stay together long term, through all the challenges of a long-term commitment. Your body language may well seem quite low-key. You may not gaze deep into your partner's eyes or talk in loving tones, because you no longer need to show how infatuated you are. But you no longer (or only rarely) row with your partner, because you have both come to a working arrangement about the ways you disagree.

And you will both unconsciously match each other's posture, gestures or even breathing patterns on a minute-to-minute level. You will be able to read each other's body language right down to the last blink. And you will have a series of personal body language codes that you use to communicate only with each other – for issues as different as when to have sex through to when to leave a party.

Your body language will be in contented synchrony – in nonverbal terms, you will act not as two individuals, but as an integrated and happy unit.

What One Body Language Strategy Can I Best Use in Order to Improve My Long-term Partnership?

The answer to this question is a single word: Touch. For of all the different kinds of body language, touch is the one that in Western society gets most ignored and most neglected.

When you start a relationship, you show your partner by all kinds of body language signals that you like her (or him) and want to be with her. You show this by looking, listening, smiling – and touching a great deal. As the relationship continues and develops, and you both get more secure with each other, many of these body language signals fade. But while you will still always look, listen and smile, often you stop touching your partner completely – unless you are having sex. An otherwise committed couple may only touch each other once or twice a week outside the bedroom.

The problem with this is that touching and being touched are essential to humans. Touch was our most important sense early in life and it still is vital when we grow up. Touch releases the hormone oxytocin into the blood stream making us feel safe, comforting us , helping us to feel better about ourselves. It actually

keeps us healthy. Couples who don't touch, who never make love or cuddle, tend to develop irritability, depression and even high blood pressure.

Touching also bonds you to your partner. Oxytocin creates strong bodily sensations: you literally feel more for a person you can touch and do touch. Recent research has shown that couples who fall asleep wrapped in each other's arms tend to feel more positive about each other than those who do not have that 'touch down' time. (The same study showed that couples who have argued during the day and want to make up tend to move unconsciously together during night-time sleep, as if literally moving closer will bring them closer emotionally.)

So touch more. Start with an early morning cuddle. Hug each other goodbye as you go to work. Offer a similar hug of welcome when you meet again. And rather than sit in separate chairs, curl up together on the sofa in the evenings.

Do not be afraid to touch each other in passing. Put a hand on your partner's head as you walk behind her chair; place an arm round your partner's waist as you meet in the bathroom; offer a kiss over the washing up.

Also create more formal touching times. Have a bath together; go to ballroom dancing classes; take it in turns to give each other a massage at night when the children are in bed. Any of these may lead to passion, but that is not the point. The point is to 'touch down' with each other as many times as you would look at each other, or listen to each other.

If you do, and if you can continue to touch with admiration, affection and passion, then your bodies and your body language will continue to reflect your love for each other throughout your long and happy lives.

5 ♥ Total Strangers

How Can Body Language Help Me When I Am in Public?

The fascination – and the challenge – of public situations is that you are among strangers. Whether in a queue, at a concert, or on a train, everyone around you is in his or her own little world. It is hard to make contact. Whether you enjoy being in public, or feel uneasy, body language can help because it gives you a 'way in'.

If you are interested in other people, then body language gives you an accurate tool to analyse what is going on around you. The nonverbal signals of public spaces and public gatherings are different from private body language, but just as easily interpreted. It is intriguing to watch as people act out public patterns of behaviour, behave differently because they are in a crowd and get drawn into doing things that they would never do alone. And whether you are in a rush or have time to kill, being aware of all this will help you understand human nature just a little more.

You can also use body language in individual interactions. For when you are in public, you are constantly creating relationships with people you do not know and will never meet again – in shops, on buses, in pubs. You can use body language skills to read people's intentions. You can use it to create good relationships with them, however temporary those relationships are. You can use it to block contact with them if that contact feels uncomfortable to you.

In fact, being in public can create dangers that just do not exist when you are on home ground. By using body language to avoid and prevent these situations, where words just are not possible or would not make an impact, you can actually feel safer. And in the end, if something risky does happen, you can even use body language to escape from it – or to cope with it.

What Is Different About Body Language in a Shopping Mall?

Public streets, full of tiny shops in the open air where people and traffic take up the same space and sometimes have to compete in order to survive, have created a very particular body language pattern – particularly in the colder countries of the Northern hemisphere.

With the arrival of the mall, the indoor shopping centre, everything has changed. Given a roof over our heads, a traffic-free zone, central heating in the winter and air-conditioning in the summer, suddenly we have adopted the shopping body language of Mediterranean countries.

So, for example, the walking pace of shoppers in a mall is noticeably slower than on the street; people stroll rather than hurry. The architects have supplied walkways five times as wide as normal pavements, so groups of several people walk and talk together, rather than only two abreast at a time. Because of the lack of traffic, parents are happier for their children to run ahead, wander to one side, lag behind. The pace of movement is more relaxed, more informal, less 'directed'.

We are also more likely to stop in a mall. There are more seats, less chance of frostbite. So we will stop to chat, eat a snack, check a lottery ticket. We will also be more likely to watch people, for while on the street it is usually only those with time on their hands – the old and the young – who sit and stare: in shopping malls everyone does it. The age range is much wider, the time spent watching much longer.

On the other hand, we do not window shop much in malls. Windows are not as important as they are on the street, where the only way to get you inside a shop is to tempt you by a window display. In the mall, windows are so unimportant that some shops have removed them altogether in favour of huge entrance doors which not only let you see the goods, but give you direct access to them.

And whereas outdoors, most stores have automatic doors to keep heating costs down, in malls the entrances are always open. So rather than rush from one purchase to another, in malls we will wander into and out of stores, not really having to make a decision to enter a shop because we do not have to open a door. Sneakily, too, the floor pattern or carpeting of mall shops is designed to look the same as that of the public walkway flooring, to make the distinction between shops and 'street' less noticeable and so tempt you into the shops themselves.

Which is best, street or mall? Because malls are generally more relaxed places to be, they are easier to shop in, more fun – in a word, warmer. But you are more likely to spend more time and more cash there. So, quite literally, you pay your money and you take your choice.

What Is 'Trolley Body Language'?

If a car is an extension of people's personality on the road, then the shopping trolley or cart is the extension of their personality in the supermarket.

Some shoppers are tentative, edging round corners, always hanging back, meeting a 'traffic jam' apologetically and wiggling their way through it; perhaps they are nervous, careful people who lack self-confidence. Then there are the 'ram raiders' who charge through the supermarket banging into other people's trolleys and then simply carrying on; perhaps these are aggressive people, or perhaps they are shopping in their lunch-hour and have a deadline to meet.

The 'park and ride' shoppers place their trolleys at significant points in the shop and then bring their goods back to these central collecting points. They tend to be organized and, if parents, send all the children off on collection duty, to halve the shopping time. Finally, notice the 'kerb crawlers' who hug the side of the frozen food cabinets, poring over the goods; they may be people who have time to shop slowly, or who have to check prices and relative quality before making any decisions.

If two people are in charge of the trolley, problems multiply. They both feel responsible, they both want to feel in control, and that may make them confrontational. Such trolley wars can occur when one person is pushing but the other keeps hijacking the trolley to different aisles. They can occur when one person is pushing and the other 'lends a hand' unconsciously, slowing the trolley down and altering its direction. And when choosing goods, the trolley can become the battle front line; one person puts something in, the other takes it out, then they stand each side of the trolley and brandish the items across it.

Then comes the checkout. Lone shoppers may display more tension at the checkout than anywhere else, as they try to do everything single-handed – fumble with cheque books, rush their packing, shoot apologetic glances at the people behind them in the queue. Pairs, meanwhile, still find opportunities for conflict – as one is left to unload the trolley while the other goes to get forgotten items; or as one loads the bags while the other hovers at the till and seems to be doing nothing.

How can you personally avoid problems? Watch out for your nonverbal signs of tension: fast, uncoordinated movements; stiff, tense shoulders; white-knuckled hands on the trolley handle. If on your own, slow down and try to shake off any muscle tension. If with a companion, try making physical contact; a pat of your hand or a 'grooming gesture' on the back of your companion's neck can reduce tension instantly. Then divide responsibility – just one person pushing at any one time will guarantee fewer battles. And if you both want control, simply swap roles halfway round the aisles.

How Can I Get Good Service from a Sales Assistant?

When you interact with a sales assistant, you have just a few minutes to create a working relationship and use that to make a successful purchase. In fact, many shop assistants are trained to use body language to support you – but you can help too by using your own nonverbal skills.

As you enter the shop, look for the assistant who has the most effective body language, one who is alert and looks friendly and confident. Steer clear if, as she (or he) interacts with other staff or customers, she looks nonverbally overpushy or completely uninterested. For clothes shopping in particular, you may also want to take the advice of some 'style guides' which suggest that when choosing an assistant you opt for one who has roughly your build and colouring; she will instinctively know, from her knowledge of her own body, what suits you.

Once you have made contact with the most appropriate assistant, put some nonverbal effort into the first few seconds of the interaction. Shop staff so often get treated like a lower form of life that if you make eye contact, smile and pass a comment in a friendly voice, this will immediately relax the assistant and make things more likely to go well.

As you start to look at possible purchases, use your body language to back up rather than to undermine what you are saying. If you want information, for example, use the nonverbal combination of head tilt, questioning smile and raised eyebrows which indicates an interested need to know more; this set of signals is designed to encourage other people to feel good about explaining something.

If you do not want to make a purchase, be clear about that too. It can be tempting to give 'unsure' signals, with your head tilting to one side then the other, a wiggle of your shoulders, a twist of the mouth and hesitation in your voice; somehow these signs seem kinder and less rejecting than a definite no. The problem here is that a trained sales assistant, faced with 'unsure' signals, will automatically try to persuade you. If you are certain you do not want something, and do not want to be pressured, get eye contact, shake your head and use a firm voice.

On the other hand, if the assistant presents you with something you want, then show your appreciation clearly. A thank you, accompanied by a smile of approval, will not only make the assistant delighted that you are pleased but will also lay the groundwork for getting good service next time you enter the store.

What Is 'the Flinch' and How Can It Reduce the Price of a Car?

Salespeople who specialize in big purchases can be intimidating. They depend on your sale for their commission – so they can pressure you to buy on their terms rather than the ones you want. But it does not have to be like this.

Begin by approaching the salesperson confidently. An obviously nervous customer can make a salesperson act even more aggressively, and this is not a good basis for negotiation. Instead, show your willingness to be friendly, with a smile and eye contact, a handshake and an amiable tone of voice. Create a bond between you that will relax you both.

Then, take your time to find out about the product – the different models of car, for example. Continue to be friendly; you will get better information and sales service that way. If you like the product, show this with genuine smiles, warmth in your voice and nods of approval – it is a myth that seeming uncertain about a purchase will cause the salesperson to lower the price.

But then, as you move towards the sale and have shown clearly that you really do want the car or other major item, change your approach. Remember that salespeople have to be natural extroverts to succeed in their job. And extroverts thrive on other people's friendly approval – but wilt when faced with disapproval. They will be motivated by pleasing you, urged on by the threat of your displeasure.

So with the sale looming, remove your approval. Let your smile fade, your nods stop, your warm tone disappear. Turn your head slightly away. Frown slightly in disapproval. Shake your head at the price. Let your voice drop in disappointment. In the trade this is known as the 'flinch' – where the customer shows the salesperson that he (or she) has to try that little bit harder. With your friendly body language withdrawn, the salesperson is left feeling bad – and desperately wanting to please you in order to gain the sale.

Then, give him a way to please. Say quite clearly what it is you want – part exchange, a lower price, extended credit. If he is able to provide this, then smile again, put the warmth back into your voice, reach out and give him a congratulatory pat on the shoulder.

If the salesperson is not able to give you what you want, only then do you have to consider whether you are willing to buy anyway. Very often you may decide to do just that – to buy the car, the fridge, or the double glazing at the original price. But flinching is always worth a try. It may work – and if it doesn't, you have lost nothing.

What Really Happens When I Am in the Cinema?

When you go to see a film, you don't simply sit and watch it. In fact, all your body language changes, on the inside as well as on the outside, because without knowing it you are being hypnotized. You may think that hypnosis is some mysterious mental magic, where a stage hypnotist convinces you that you are somewhere else, being someone else. But in fact a hypnotic trance occurs when, focused on one particular thing, you lose track of what is happening in the real world and your body responds by taking on a whole new form of behaviour, externally and internally. In fact, most of us enter into a mild trance state many times a day – when driving the car, day-dreaming, using a computer. Going to the movies is physiologically just one stage on from this. You are seated in a dark room with no distractions from people, telephones, pets – or the possibility of getting up to make a cup of coffee. In this situation all you have to do is to concentrate on what is in front of you. And in front of you, filling your vision and so filling your mind, are large, bright, moving objects – the images on the screen. Your eyes focus on these, and become so focused that you lose awareness of yourself.

And as you focus so completely, your physiology naturally shifts. You blink less, your breathing rate goes down, your heart rate drops. You are in a different state from normal; a state much more similar to sleep than to being awake – a state of hypnotic trance.

But also, when you are in this state, the film on the screen can affect your body so completely that you almost experience what you see as real. So cinema audiences shift fractionally along with on-screen movement, squaring their shoulders before the big fight, jerking in terror when the monster appears. They do this in synchrony with the screen characters, moving within 1/48th of a second of their heroes, and in perfect rhythm with them.

And this body language identification is not just on the outside. If you identify with the characters, your internal body language alters too – your muscles, nervous system, heart rate and blood-pressure respond almost as if you were actually in the film yourself. As the hero faces the baddie, your heart rate quickens and your mouth goes dry. As the heroine yearns for her lover, you feel tears coming to your eyes.

For an hour or so you actually believe, mentally and physically, that you are somewhere else, being someone else. You may think you are at the movies. But your body – and your body language – think differently.

How Can Body Language Help Me Get Served in the Pub?

You are standing at the bar in a pub, waiting to be served. The bar staff ignore you. Are you invisible? If so, what can you do? In fact, because of the noise in most pubs, good bar staff get much of their information from nonverbal cues. The secret of getting served in a pub is to realize this and make it work for you.

When you get to the bar, claim your 'territory'. If you do not you may simply get lost in the group of customers who are standing at the bar to drink rather than to order. They will tend to turn sideways or backwards, facing out towards the room. You, on the contrary, should move right up to the bar, rest both elbows on it and face directly inwards to claim your space.

Next, make it clear that you have not been served and want to be. Focus all your attention on the bar person in order to get her (or his) attention. 'Track' her with your body, following her as she moves by turning your shoulders, head and eyes towards her. Do not look away, even for a moment, or you may lose the opportunity to catch her eye. When you do, hold your money visibly in your hand and above bar level, and use that very particular facial expression that both expects and accuses: head tilted on one side, raised eyebrows, closed-mouth smile.

What if you do not get noticed? It is almost certainly because you are using the wrong body language, therefore giving bar staff the wrong information. Turning away from the bar can seem to indicate that you have already been served. Not holding money may give the impression that you want attention but not in order to buy something – so the staff will tend to deprioritize you. Not looking worried may signal that you have not been waiting that long, or that you are not next in the queue; the bar person will turn to someone else.

(Interestingly, in a British pub, the body language of indignation, such as raising your voice, waving your money or screwing up your face in anger, may actually mean staff will ignore you because you are making them feel too pressured!)

How will you know you have been spotted? The bar person will give you eye contact plus one of a number of acknowledgement signals such as a double raised-eyebrow 'flash', a nod or a raised finger. You need to acknowledge this in return with a nod and smile. Then, in fact, as long as you keep facing the bar to signal you are still 'on hold', you can stop trying. Miraculously, when the next drink is served, it will be yours!

What is the Nonverbal Difference between Different Kinds of Restaurants?

When it comes to dining out, there is a sliding scale between low-price places and high-price places. The differences are not only in what you eat and how good the food is, but in the subtle 'scene setting': the nonverbal cues of decor, layout and table arrangement; the body language staff use; the body language you use to them.

Let us start with one of the basics – freedom of movement. You might think that the more you pay, the more liberty you get – but no. At a roadside café or stand, your freedom of movement is complete – you park where you want, wander across, take your food, disappear into the night. At a motorway service station you are slightly more restricted, funnelled into and out of a food area where several bays offer a choice, but left to your own devices when choosing a table. Compare this with a top-class restaurant, where you are met at the door, marched across to a table chosen for you, seated and largely kept in your place. The aim is that better-paying customers do not have to move; the result is that your freedom is restricted.

The other result is that the staff themselves move much more in order to deliver the food – and, as a result, move into your personal space. At a low-price eaterie the staff keep well back – behind a counter for self-service, behind a window in a drive-in burger place. In a medium-level restaurant they come right up to your table with the dishes but then back off and leave you to help yourself. In a 'silver service' establishment, where waiters do everything, they lean round you, across you, between you – moving into your 'intimate' space of 45 cm (18 in) in a way you would normally only allow children and lovers to do!

There is a potential problem here: Human beings feel invaded if unknown people get too close, so the closer service staff are to you, the more threatened you might feel – if they tried to be at all personal. So waiters' nonverbal approach balances out any possible problems. Where staff physically keep their distance, body language can often be quite informal; waiters can smile in a friend-ly fashion, joke, let their posture and gestures be very familiar, face you directly as an equal. Where staff move close, waiters need to be like wallpaper if they are not to intrude on your evening. So they dress in neutral colours, avoid your line of sight, come up behind you to serve, keep their expressions blank and their voices low and calm.

When you leave, though, the whole relationship shifts. You exit from a burger stand without being noticed. You leave with a mini-mum of interaction from a pizza place, where the bill is left on your table for you to present at the till in your own time. But the high-er the price, the more prolonged and personal the parting. At the Ritz, the waiters present your bill, fetch and carry your credit card, get the receipt, bring your coat, pour you endless 'final' cups of cof-fee. It is as if, having been so close to you for so many hours, the staff just cannot bear to let you go!

Which Three Agendas Do People Have When They Go Swimming?

Swimming pools are not just for swimming. People have all kinds of reason for going. Next time you are there, watch out for these three agendas...

Serious swimmers use body language which signals they have a job to do; they are not there for the people. So they will tend to arrive alone, walking briskly in past the turnstiles with a bare smile and nod of greeting at the resident staff. They will find a quiet corner of the changing room – they know just where to go because they are probably here every day. They will change quickly, often having their costumes on under their clothes for speed.

Once in the water they will immediately settle to a regular pace, doing many lengths using the same stroke. They will make hardly any noise. They will never stop to play. They will steer well clear of flumes, wave machines or other distractions. And when resting, or out of the water, they will not look around or approach others. Their lack of expression and eye contact will reveal that they are far more interested in what is going on with their own bodies than with anyone else's – they are concentrating on the sensations of swimming, not on the fun of the pool.

In direct contrast, playful swimmers are only there for the fun. They go in large family or friendship groups, of varying ages and genders, and they will chat, joke, laugh and jostle as they drift up to the turnstiles. In the changing room, they will 'annex' a section of the lockers, taking up a lot of space and often making a lot of noise. Then they will go out as a group into the swimming area and spread over a randomly selected section of 'territory', seats or poolside area.

Playful swimmers will spend almost as much time in the water as serious swimmers, but in a very different way. Their body language will be highly energetic, with lots of movement, noise and touch to show they are close. They will jump, dive or throw things from person to person in the water, but hardly ever swim for more than a few strokes. But, like the serious swimmers, playful swimmers will not gaze around them much. They are not looking to make new friends; they have enough of their own.

Then, there are the swimming groupies. These are almost always young people, and for them the pool is really a theatre for the teenage ritual of 'posing and picking up'. They will go every single day during the school holidays, until they are old enough to pair off and want to be alone – after which they may never go swimming ever again. Groupies, male and female, will arrive in small, same-sex groups. They will greet the resident staff like the good friends they often are, spend time in the changing room preparing in front of the mirror, then emerge onto the swimming pool stage.

Groupies have their own dedicated space, often near where the staff are based, which they occupy every day. There they will sit, stand, chat, smile – and 'display' in order to attract attention. Do they look around? Yes, all the time, to check who is watching, to 'accidentally' catch someone's eye. Do they go in the water? Only occasionally, and then usually only when, as an excuse for adolescent loveplay, someone throws someone else in. For this group – except as a backdrop to the fascinating games they are playing – the water itself simply is not important at all!

What Is Interesting About Religious Body Language?

Whether or not you are a believer, the body language of religious worship is fascinating because it reflects such a great deal both about the religion and about the worshippers.

Most religions, for example, suggest that each believer should have a personal religious practice. There will be a recognized body language for this. If the believer needs to worship a deity which is seen as superior, then you will find people kneeling, perhaps with hands joined and pointing towards the heaven where, in medieval times, the deity was believed to reside.

Or, if the key act of individual religion is to repeat and learn sacred scripture, then body language may help with this, involving an upright position so that the person can chant easily, along with some rocking or bowing to keep a rhythm which helps the worshiper memorize the relevant verses.

If a central part of one's religious observation is meditation, with concentration on one's own body and not outside distractions, then the body language will include a special meditation posture. This will probably involve keeping the spine straight and the head erect to create a sensation of balance and calm, closed eyes to shut off outside input, and some sort of concentration aid such as a rosary which keeps fingers busy and allows the mind to go free.

Most religions involve group worship – and this too is a nonverbal reflection of belief. In traditional Western, Christian culture, for example, churches have often been built as the biggest, tallest building in a community, designed to show the importance and power of the deity. A church's focus is its altar, with a surrounding area where only celebrants are allowed, and beyond that a larger space for the 'ordinary' congregation. The celebrants – priest, altar boys, choir – dress in splendid costumes which mark them out as special. They will use large, directive gestures which, even from one end of a huge cathedral to the other, show the congregation what to do.

The congregation, obeying these directions, follow a definite pattern of movement. They stand – which gives the lungs more breathing power for singing or praying out loud. They sit – which allows physical support during a prolonged sermon. They kneel – again reflecting the belief in a king-like deity when praying. Throughout the service, everyone's body language is controlled, restrained, respectful and focused on the deity.

But as Christianity has moved towards a more 'people-centred' approach towards the end of the twentieth century, body language has changed to reflect this. So churches may now be circular to reflect equality among all people. Celebrants may dress in everyday clothes, hardly different from those of their congregation. Services may encourage spontaneity and freedom of movement. They may include physical activity such as singing or dancing, not only because it is now realized that such movement gives people a positive feeling physiologically, but also because believers increasingly see human expression as being positive, a reflection of the glory of their god.

And, finally, many services will now include not only an opportunity for direct contact with the deity, through prayer, but also direct contact with the community, with some part of the service incorporating handshakes, kisses or hugs among members of the congregation.

What Is the Basic Body Language of Cars?

Cars may be mechanical objects but they have their own body language, albeit manipulated by their drivers. And, like humans, cars have conscious and unconscious body language – deliberate, controlled, but not necessarily truthful signals, and those signals that reveal the driver's real intentions because they are unconscious and uncontrollable.

A car's conscious body language comes from its lights – which of course are specifically designed for 'signalling'. The back lights are there for other road users, indicating a car's movements; through them you get the answers to many questions. Is a car going to stop? – Check its brake lights. Is it going to reverse? – See the reversing lights. Is there an emergency ahead? – See the emergency lights flashing on and off. Is the car going to turn left or right? – Look for the indicator lights, which of course are a replacement for the literal body language of a hand waving out of a window.

The front headlights are actually only designed to light up the road ahead for the driver. But they are also used in an informal lights 'language' that is not in the Highway Code, and though not strictly legal, is nevertheless used by many drivers. These lights can show that another car is letting you go first – as when you are turning right and the car coming towards you flashes its lights. They are used to say 'Hello!' – as when two vans from the same firm flash their headlights as they pass. They are used to tell you there is a problem – as when you set off at night and another car 'blinks' to tell you that you have not switched your lights on. And they are used to signal that it is safe – as when on a motorway a lorry flashes to encourage you to pull in after overtaking (the 'thank you' signal in return consists of a single flash of your left, then right, then left rear indicators.)

But all these conscious, controlled driving signals are often misleading – for a driver can signal one thing and do something completely different. The unconscious body language signs of driving, on the other hand, are the position of the front wheels. These tell you not what the driver thinks she is doing, but what she really is doing – going right, going left, aiming to park, about to do a U-turn. Though the driver is largely unaware of where her front wheels are, they reveal her intentions precisely – even down to when she changes her mind in the middle of a manoeuvre.

So if you really want to understand the body language of a car – more important, if you really want to predict just what a driver is going to do next – watch the car's unconscious rather than its conscious signals!

How Can I Tell When Another Driver Is About to Do Something Dangerous?

Every driver has his own 'safety zone', driving conditions and driving style within which he will drive safely. And it is possible to tell, from the way someone drives, when he is within his safety zone – or whether he is in a situation that is just too demanding for him.

The first possible clue is whether the driver is matching speed to the conditions. Too fast is obviously a problem; 60 miles an hour in traffic in a built-up area will not give anyone time to react within his safety zone, however good a driver he is. But interestingly, driving too slowly may also indicate that the driver is a potential danger. Driving below the pace of other traffic may indicate that he is nervous or unsure, and so likely to make mistakes.

Driving too close to other cars may mean that a driver is particularly aggressive, or in a hurry – which will make him careless. Too far back, unless he is signalling a manoeuvre, can indicate a timid or sleepy driver.

Another danger signal is if a driver seems to be ignoring road signs. If so, his mental state or the road conditions are probably such that he is not taking in the information he needs to. Beware if a driver straddles the white line, seems to notice a pedestrian crossing only at the last moment, or fails to slow down when he should.

If a driver gives contradictory signals, he may be confused by the road situation. So a car ahead of you indicating left and moving to the right will probably turn right in the end. A car which is slowing down while the driver seems to be looking across to the left is probably about to park, even if the left indicator is not flashing. A car on a roundabout (rotary) that is not signalling at all, but which seems to be sticking to the inner lane, is probably going to come full circle and straight across your bows.

Though most of the body language of driving is actually 'car language', also keep an eye on the 'body' of the driver ahead or the one next to you at the traffic lights. Look out for the driver who continuously turns his head to talk to his passenger, one whose noticeable movements indicate that he is very emotional, one who continuously leans down to change the tape in the cassette player. All these distractions may mean he is unsafe to be near.

In all these situations, you have to decide what to do. Your first line of defence will be the classic one of slowing down slightly and covering the brake. Next, be aware of all the possible manoeuvres the suspect driver might make, and think ahead about what your best response could be.

If the situation seems serious – if you suspect that the driver ahead of you is actually asleep, for example – then your best course of action may well be to turn off and, if you are genuinely concerned about the driver's (and others') safety, get in touch with the police or motorway authorities.

What Is 'Road Rage' and How Can It Kill?

All of us get irritated from time to time, particularly when we are feeling threatened or stressed. Studies of emotion reveal that irritation affects the human body very dramatically. Our whole nervous system goes into action, so that blood rushes to our brain, adrenalin floods our system, our heart rate, breathing and blood-pressure increase; in short, we prepare for action.

If this action does not take place, if we simply ignore the sensations of anger, then we feel very uncomfortable indeed. The most helpful answer is to reduce the discomfort, perhaps by relaxation or exercise, and then deal calmly with whatever is causing the irritation.

In a car, irritation can build up quite quickly as other people's driving starts to annoy because it threatens us. Particularly if we are in a bad mood to start with – as many people are when they leave the house in the morning to drive to work, or leave work in the evening to drive home – our bodies react speedily with the above-mentioned uncomfortable sensations.

The problem is that in a car we cannot easily reduce our discomfort. We cannot get other people to drive differently. We may not want to stop the car and take some exercise. So the feelings build up. Eventually what we feel is 'road rage'.

When someone drives in a way that restricts or endangers our own progress, we may mutter under our breath or shout obscenities in the direction of the other driver. We may take it further, shaking a fist, putting up two fingers, looking across into the other car with angry, staring eye contact to try to make our point. Road rage can make us want to take even more dramatic action, getting out of our car at the lights, hammering on the other driver's window, even opening the door and attacking her.

Though all of these angry reactions are dangerous, they are not the real killers. More dangerous is when we stop expressing our anger through our own body language, and start expressing it through our car's nonverbal signals. If we drive on when we are really angry, then we can put ourselves and others in real danger.

Our vision may narrow, meaning that we do not notice road signs or the manoeuvres of other cars. Our impression of speed may be inaccurate, meaning that we drive faster and carry out manoeuvres at a higher speed. We may misjudge distances, cutting down the space between us and the car in front, or imagining we can squeeze through a gap that is too narrow. We may let emotion override our judgement, and therefore start flashing lights, carving people up, even deliberately aiming to nudge other cars, without any real sense of how dangerous this can be.

Because of all this, for our own sakes and everyone else's, it is better to pull over for a few minutes and strangle a lamp-post rather than simply carry on driving when we feel 'road rage'.

How Can I Cope with Officials?

There is a certain kind of body language which officials are trained to use. And if you are dealing with ticket inspectors, police officers and traffic wardens, then it is as well first to understand these very particular nonverbal cues, and then be able to cope with them.

The mark of authority figures is often the uniform they wear, which echoes military power and status. So doormen and ward matrons alike often wear dark uniforms, in black, blue or green, with metal badges and a helmet or cap that not only gives an impression of formality but also adds height.

Along with all this, authority figures usually develop status body language. They will stand or sit erect, their shoulders back and with a set, slightly expressionless face. They will avoid uncontrolled gestures, signals of friendship such as broad smiles, and slightly quirky behaviour such as a wink or a giggle. Their voices will be steady and strong, their tone formal and polite.

In response to all this, even in situations where we are not under threat in any way, many of us do become nervous. Somehow, faced with all these body language signals of power and status, we start to feel inferior or even slightly guilty. We may look down submissively, start stuttering or stammering, make little 'escape movements' with our hands or feet, and bite our lips as if to stop ourselves saying something we might regret. One study showed that at the approach of a police officer, both women and men used protective gestures – arms across the body or hands instinctively moving to protect the crotch!

Instead of becoming nervous when faced with authority like this – whether stopped by a ticket inspector or faced with a traffic warden – the key is to keep calm. You need, of course, to show in your body language that you acknowledge the presence of authority, so you may choose not to stare directly at the official, leap up in a confrontational way, or talk in a loud and argumentative tone. But equally, it is as well not to seem so nervous that you arouse suspicion, nor so friendly that you seem to be trying to distract the official from the matter in hand.

Instead, relax as much you can. Breathe slowly and steadily to allow your body to calm down. Stay seated unless asked to get up, then stand easily with your head slightly tilted so as not to seem challenging. Keep a pleasant expression and answer any questions in an untroubled but not jokey tone of voice.

Finally, when your ticket is clipped or your driving licence checked to the official's satisfaction, you may notice a mental 'signing off' process. You are obviously not a danger, so the body language of authority relaxes just slightly. In response, you can also be more at ease – though not too much more – acting just slightly more informal to reflect the fact that although this is an authority figure, he now realizes that he does not need to assert his authority over you.

Why Do People Set Up Home Every Time They Travel on a Train?

Human beings like the security of knowing that they have their own space – even in situations where, in fact, everything is public property. Look at passengers on a train. If the journey is to be a relatively long one, there is more need to have a safe 'home base'. Acknowledging this, train designers have provided four-seat bays which lend themselves very easily to the creation of little territories.

Watch, then, for passengers 'house-hunting'. They may already have formally reserved their space; but if not, they will walk down the train, outside or inside, choosing a spot that fulfils their needs. Is the bay facing the engine, is it near the buffet, near the toilet, is it smoking or non-smoking? Is it a two-seater bay, which gives more privacy but less space, or a four-seater where someone else will come along to share? Once chosen, 'territory' will be marked: coat on luggage rack, bag on seat and something on the table to make absolutely sure that no one intrudes.

If passengers who know each other are sharing a bay, they will feel able to spread out across the table. But if strangers are sharing, there will be a nonverbal negotiation about territory not only on but also under the table. Both passengers shift papers, move food and drink, cross and uncross legs – all to the accompaniment of sideways glances and reassuring smiles – until both are satisfied that they have what they need. This could be that each person gives up all the room because he or she does not want it – or it could be that there is a mental dotted line down the middle of the table that marks the division between each person's space.

And within that space, passengers will actually feel able to do many of the things that they do at home. They will eat. They will sleep. They will read. If a group is sitting together, they will talk, play games, drink beer. They will apply makeup and do their hair. They will work on business papers, use a calculator, talk into a portable phone, type into a computer.

It is not just that there is space for all these activities – the leg room provided is similar to that on an underground train. It is not just that there is a table provided – restaurants have these but diners do not annex them in quite the same way. It is that, insecure in the way only travellers can be, passengers need to feel they have a place which, even for just the few hours they are travelling, is Home Sweet Home.

How Do People Use Body Language to Survive on a Rush-hour Tube Train?

On the London Underground, people are regularly, consistently, inexorably pressed up against other people every day. So it is not surprising that Tube commuters, like all humans in crowded and static situations, use a particular set of nonverbal strategies simply in order to survive.

The natural human response to strangers is to keep our distance. But in a crowded train carriage, we simply cannot. So we have to protect ourselves: We put up barriers, using shoulder bags and brief cases held in front of our bodies or, failing that, using crossed arms or hands held at crotch height. We read newspapers and magazines to prevent eye contact with others; if there is room, we open our papers out so that we can hide behind them even further. We hunch our shoulders as if not hearing what is going on around us. So as not to invite approaches, we will seem unapproachable, staring through people, keeping our expressions blank and unsmiling, making no contact at all.

As well as to give self-protection, Tube body language has also developed to indicate that we are not threatening to other people. So we take up as little space as possible, tucking in elbows and bags so as not to make contact, bowing our heads slightly in the age-old submissive movement that tells other people we are not going to make trouble. When new people enter the carriage, we shift slightly, as if to make room for them, even if in actual fact there is nowhere to shift to. If we have to press up against someone, then we shrug and smile apologetically as if to say that it is not really our fault.

All these behaviours work quite well – until things get just too much. It is a hot day, just one too many squeezes in past the sliding doors, and all of a sudden the body language alters. We become nervous, turning this way and that as if looking for a way out. We finger our collars as if trying to breathe more easily. We start to fidget, making little 'escape movements' with our fingers in place of the running movements we really want to make with our feet.

Happily, it usually all stops there, as at the next station the carriage empties somewhat – and our body language moves back to normal again.

How Do Airports Use Nonverbal Cues to Make Life Easier?

Consider the challenge that airports face: Every day, hundreds of thousands of passengers need to be channelled from the checkout desks where they arrive, through to the planes on which they depart. How can that best happen? The secret is in creating the right environment, one that nonverbally guides yet also reassures.

You arrive at an airport. You may be nervous; studies reveal that air travellers perform ten times more anxiety gestures, such as rechecking tickets, than train travellers do.

You will probably head straight for the check-in desks. There, you are greeted by a member of the airline staff who gives you body language signals that combine two things: efficiency (an authoritative uniform, formal language and directive gestures) and friendliness (direct eye contact and a broad smile). The aim of this combination is to make you feel first secure and then calm – maybe airport staff do not want you panicking before or during the flight.

The check-in desks not only make you feel safe. They also relieve you of your baggage, which means that you can move about easily. This is a practical strategy, and one that also means that you are not tempted to wander away from the airport – which now has your belongings – and so delay your flight. You are freed up to wander round. You have certainly got time to do this; your pre-flight nerves, along with your pre-flight instructions, mean that you may well have arrived anything up to two and a half hours before your plane takes off.

During that two and a half hours, what are you likely to do, in your anxious state? You will want to eat (humans often eat to steady their nerves), and you may want to buy all the things that you think you may have forgotten (another documented reaction to anxiety). And guess what? – Airports deliberately provide ample opportunities to eat and shop – and, outside the departure lounge at any rate, not much opportunity simply to sit and wait. Sneaky, huh?

After a while, however, airports become keen to divide off people who are travelling from those in the airport for other reasons. They want to complete the time-consuming pre-flight checks – such as security and passport control – just in case something goes wrong. They want to move you a little nearer to your flight, so that you will be more likely to be in the right place at the right time. So they call you, well in advance, into the departure lounge. This is smaller, not only because fewer people use it, but also because it is not so filled with shops which might make it likely that you would miss the call to your gate.

When you are called to the boarding gate, you become part of an even more tightly specified group – this time, of passengers who are flying on a particular plane. You are placed in a separate lounge where you have absolutely nothing to do – so that when you are finally allowed to board, no one has the slightest excuse to be distracted, and no one goes missing at the last moment.

Finally, you hand in your boarding pass and walk onto the plane. And at this point, the airport staff heave a sigh of relief. Their nonverbal strategies have succeeded in getting you successfully on the plane and off their hands. Happy landing!

What Is the Body Language of Queuing?

The body language of queuing has really only developed since the Second World War. Before that, people simply gathered in a random way at bus stops or in shop doorways. Then when a bus arrived or a shop opened, they stepped forward in any order. This rather casual attitude to taking your turn came not only from a much more leisurely lifestyle, but also from a belief that there was enough for everybody. Rationing and the war changed that belief – now, queuing is a part of life.

The classic post-war 'line' queue happens when people spontaneously stand one behind another. It is usually found in shops and supermarkets; people stand strictly in place, slightly closer than they normally would to a stranger, as if to make the queue look shorter. You will see irritated movements if someone at the front of the queue takes longer than the average time for his transaction. But people will rarely talk because they are too busy checking their own queue to see how fast it is moving, too busy looking around at other queues to see if it is worthwhile 'swapping'. If it is, there will be a sudden flurry of activity, as some people swap, others debate whether to swap, and yet others start to swap and then stay where they are.

The 'funnelled' queue is a recent development. It is found in service buildings such as banks and libraries, and consists of a series of waist-high tapes which first guide you into a single queue, then direct you from there to a number of service points. Body language here is different from the classic queue because there is little possibility of speeding up the process, or of competing for a place in other queues. So people in funnelled queues are in general much less tense. They do not need to keep a watching eye out, so they will talk much more, and in a much more informal way. They will be more co-operative – pointing out to the person in front that it is his turn to be served; helping others move prams or shopping baskets forward.

Recently, there has been a return to pre-war days, with far more 'random queues', particularly in outdoor situations such as at bus stops. Here, new arrivals look round at others to check who is there before them and to signal to others that they know their place in the queue – in supermarkets this process is often controlled by giving you a ticket to mark your place in, for example, the delicatessen line. Once someone has given this 'look around' signal, he can move about quite casually, wandering quite far away from the bus stop without losing his 'place'.

When the bus arrives, if there are seats for all, people move forward slowly and calmly with no real concern for who goes first. But if there are only a few places, then suddenly everything changes. People will rush to the front if they were there first or are desperate for a place; they will hang back if they feel that they came sufficiently late not to be likely to get a place; they will tackle queue-jumpers severely with sharp elbows and an angry tone of voice.

Then, as the bus fills up and drives away, anyone left behind to wait for the next one calms down – and once again people scatter randomly about until the next bus comes.

What Can I Do to Make Sure I Do Not Get into a Fight in Public?

The first step in avoiding a fight is spotting the problem before it starts. Be wary, for example, of any situation where alcohol is flowing, as this increases aggression. Be wary too of an overheated environment, such as a crowded pub or disco; when temperatures rise, so do tempers.

Watch out too for body language that tells you when people are likely to be dangerous. Alarm bells should ring if others seem to be using provocative body language. They may take on a strutting walk, square their shoulders, look around at possible competitors with a firm gaze that locks eye contact. These are all nonverbal signals that naturally appear just as a fight starts. By using them beforehand, without reason, people who want a fight invite violence – and the unlucky person who ends up on the floor will be the one who returns or responds to these signals. If you want to avoid being so unlucky, turn slightly away, relax your shoulders, avoid eye contact, simply ignore the invitation.

What if the possibility of a fight comes unannounced? You are in the middle of a conversation and suddenly realize that things are getting physical. You may notice the signals mentioned above, but this time they will be more pronounced because they are more personal. Watch out too for gestures that show someone is ready for action, such as arms held away from the body or fists clenching and unclenching. Be prepared for signs that your opponent's body is ready for activity, such as increased breathing, sweating, a reddening of the skin. Be particularly wary of sudden paleness – which is a sure sign that the body is on the point of action.

The most useful thing to do at this stage is to use the body language of non-confrontation. Of course, you may feel that you have to attack on principle – and if you want to, then go ahead. You may think that the body language of non-confrontation is the same as that of nervousness – and if you do, then you will be in for a shock, as these signals will encourage the other person to bully you.

Instead, try true non-confrontational body language. If you are heading for a fight and want to avoid it, then studies have shown that if you simply reduce your height compared to that of your opponent, this will signal that you are not up for a fight and remove much of the aggression from the situation. Slump your shoulders, bow your head, drop your eyes. Looking deeply into your beer or tying your shoelace would do the trick.

Stay in this position until your opponent has found someone else to pick on. Then, walk quietly and unobtrusively away.

What Can I Do to Make Sure I Do Not Get Mugged or Molested?

As with steering clear of a fight, avoiding muggers and molesters is firstly about being alert to the danger signs. But then, because criminals like an easy life, rather than back down, you need to make it look as if attacking you would be more trouble than it is worth.

The first nonverbal danger signal may be a risky place. Steer clear of dark, deserted areas, with plenty of spots for people to hide, such as lonely lanes and parks after dark. Bear in mind though, that unfortunately some of the worst attacks happen in broad daylight near public places.

The second danger signal may be risky people. You cannot judge from appearance – some muggers are among the best-dressed people in town. But alarm bells should ring when you are on your own and people approach you without the body language that is normally used when approaching a stranger in the street – coming from behind rather than face to face, speeding up rather than slowing down as they come close.

Can you avoid being approached like this? The bottom line is that a mugger will choose to attack someone who looks as if he (or she) will give in easily. Any nonverbal signs of fear act as a fuel to violence; even big, strong people can be victims if their body language signals that they are. So do not walk with your head down, shoulders slumped, slouching, or making nervous side-to-side eye movements. Instead, however wary you may feel, keep your head up, your gaze up, your movements alert. Look as if you would actually be able to fight back if you were attacked – clench your fists if that is what it takes to look and feel aggressively confident.

If you do feel that you are under threat, then take action that keeps you in control. If you hear footsteps behind you, walk with longer strides and more quickly, but do not break into a nervous run. Cross the road so that you have a chance to see behind you. Head straight for where there are most people – preferably a main road, but up the path of a lighted house if you are absolutely desperate.

If someone comes up to you, again stay in control. If you are seated, perhaps at a bus stop or on a station platform, get up and face your attacker. If standing, stand tall. Put a barrier such as a bench or chair between you if at all possible; if nothing is available, use a bag or briefcase held in front of you. Try to look bigger, squaring your shoulders and breathing in to enlarge your chest. Lock your gaze with that of your attacker. And however much you may feel that you might be able to talk your attacker round, do not smile, touch or enter into conversation; these things will provide a lever with which to control you. Instead, say in a loud, low firm voice 'Go away – now...' Then make as much noise as you can to attract attention and help.

Remember that attackers want easy prey. If you can convince them that you are not it, they may well go away.

What Body Language Is Worth Noticing during a Team Event?

As a spectator it is interesting to watch how the body language of a team slowly shifts throughout a game – as they gradually start to lose, or head for a win.

As the teams run on at the start of the game, they will signal just how nervous they are. Do they look serious or worried, use fiddly gestures to adjust kit and equipment, make eye contact only with each other but not with the crowd or the opposing team? If they do, then they are anxious.

Some players and coaches will be using body language 'rituals' to reduce that nervousness and create team spirit – chants, clapping, stamping feet. These work largely by making each team member 'match' or parallel the body language of the others, so that they not only feel closer but are also more likely to predict what team members are going to do and be able to respond successfully to it.

The contest starts. Of course, there will be setbacks for both sides. And some players will respond to these setbacks by using body language that is less effective: losing energy, becoming less co-ordinated, seeming less able to respond to other team members, throwing fits of temper. Other players will use setbacks to spur them on: becoming more energetic, moving faster, responding more accurately to team-mates, 'matching' others more.

In some games, a seeming setback can be turned to advantage – by using deceitful body language. If fouled, a player may start to exaggerate all the signs of injury and distress. Curling up, rolling over, bowing the head and screwing up the face all act as an unspoken appeal to the referee to take revenge on behalf of the player. Mysteriously, if the player is genuinely injured, you will rarely see any of these signs because they are not needed – and, of course, once the incident is over, these signals disappear within seconds!

When a point is scored, a successful team will celebrate. They will suddenly find a spurt of energy, so will run, leap, kick, punch the air. And, particularly in a very physical sport, they will probably touch, a very basic way humans have of celebrating. The team who has just lost a point, on the other hand, will run back to their places with heads down, without making eye contact, without touching – and will tend not to react with aggression at this point, almost as if attacking behaviour is only relevant when they are in the lead, or at least on equal terms. If they are losing, even if only temporarily, they dare not actively attack.

At the point that it becomes obvious that one team will win, each team will also display totally different nonverbal cues. The losers will be quiet, passive, solitary as they walk off the field. The winners, on the other hand, will be euphoric. They will crowd together, smiling, laughing, touching. The changing room and the showers will be full of energetic body language, noise and horseplay – as if now work is over, the team is reverting to childhood body language as they play for a while.

How Might I 'Go Mad' – and How Can I Keep Sane – in a Big Crowd?

Being with a big and active crowd – at a concert, say – can feel very good. If you feel safe, and particularly if you have something in common with all the other people, then the fact of being in close contact can excite you. If people are moving, singing or shouting rhythmically, then you can join in; 'matching' or copying movement is a positive experience for humans. You may turn to other people and talk to them, make physical contact with them by dancing together, touching or hugging. You feel close to them, united.

So far, so good. But in a crowd there may be just too much going on. There are too many people, with too many voices, too much noise and too much interaction. While this kind of interaction is stimulating, your body can go into overload – with the result that you may start to feel aggressive. Studies show that overcrowding leads our bodies to produce too much adrenalin, which can make us feel violent. And then, given that being in a crowd also leads to a sense of irresponsibility, it can be easy to find something to do with this violence. And very soon, there is the concert stampede, the football riot – and the lynch mob.

If you are in a crowd and start to feel that something is going wrong, then your first line of defence is to leave, at least for a short while. Just stepping off the dance floor or going for a walk can calm your nervous system down, make you feel less aggressive, get you more in touch with your natural sanity.

But what if you cannot leave? Edging your way out of a football crowd can be impossible, particularly if you want to see the whole of the game. A quick way of avoiding the insanity factor is to prevent yourself getting affected by the crowd. Stop moving with those around you, singing with them, shouting with them. Turn to one individual person near you, make eye contact with her (or him) and smile to make the interaction more personal. If necessary, take a break from the input by putting your hands over your ears and shutting your eyes. Calm yourself by taking deep breaths.

This may only be a temporary measure, but it can make being in a crowd a sane – rather than an insane – experience.

How Can I Make Love in Public?

It sounds outrageous. Of course you would not dream of actually making love in a crowd. But, in fact, people often do get much more physically intimate in public spots than they would do anywhere else except at home alone. They will kiss, cuddle – and more – in front of thousands of strangers in a way they would not in front of two or three friends. Why?

A key reason is that being in an anonymous group of people – in the middle of the shopping centre as well as in the back row at the movies – does alter human body language.

You may feel as if you can do more and not be noticed. This happens because members of a crowd of human beings tend not to make eye contact with those they pass; such a personal link feels far too threatening. And so because when people look around at the mass of humanity no one makes eye contact, the impression people get is that they cannot be seen. It seems as if you can do anything and not be noticed.

Also, when you are with a partner in a crowd, you automatically use body language that blocks you off from other people and creates a little world of your own. You position yourself so that you are less likely to be noticed – such as on that infamous 'back row'. You stand so that the taller one of you has his or her back to the crowd and shields the other from people's gaze. You lean into each other, face to face, eye to eye. And you build little 'tents' of clothing, so that hugs happen under the protection of two open jackets, and intimate touches take place under the protection of a coat spread across a lap.

This kind of protection and anonymity gives you the opportunity to be intimate. And it also gives you the motivation: Touching, cuddling, kissing are fun, and knowing that you are in a slightly risky situation, among all these people – even if they do not seem to be looking – adds that extra frisson. The slight fear raises your heart rate, gets your adrenalin going, makes your body more sensitive. Being in public arouses you. It feels good – so you do it.

What Is the Secret of Success When Speaking in Public?

The difference between being someone who speaks well in public and one who does not is not in the words you say. The secret of successful public speaking is much more in *how* you say those words.

Good public speakers grab the audience's attention the minute they take the floor. Their walk to the podium, or their rising to speak, are all part of the performance. So as you make your entrance walk tall, stand straight, seem confident by holding your head high, however nervous you are. Look round and make eye contact with individuals in all parts of the room.

As you begin to speak, check your posture. If you stand with your weight on one side or sit with your legs crossed, you will seem to the audience to be physically off-balance, even mentally uncertain of what you are saying. If you bend over the podium or clutch your notes on your lap, you will seem nervous and insecure. Instead, whether seated or standing, get firmly balanced, with both feet on the floor.

Use your eyes. Look up and out to the audience as much as you can; this is one reason for using minimal notes and not reading what you are going to say. Do visual 'sweeps' of the room, looking to the back left, back right, front left, front right as you speak. Then let your gaze linger on just one or two individuals in the audience and make particular contact. That way, everyone in the audience will feel that you are talking directly to her or him, and will listen intently to what you say.

Voice is obviously all important. If there is no microphone, raise the pitch of your voice slightly rather than the volume to make sure that you can be heard. Concentrate on variety, altering your speed and rhythm, allowing your voice to rise with emotion and then drop, taking a 'dramatic' pause – all these can keep the audience's interest where a flat, monotone delivery will make them fall asleep.

Also use your gestures to help you. There is no need to wave your hands like flags – but remember that gestures add emphasis, generate interest, create mood. Use a direct, downwards gesture to stress a particularly important word or phrase. Use a wide, arms-open inclusive gesture when you want your audience to agree with what you are saying. And if your speech contains emotion, then allow yourself to let your hands reflect this, perhaps clenching your fist or clasping both hands together to show how strongly you feel.

As you begin to move to the end of your speech, do not 'fade away' nonverbally. It may be tempting to rush through the last words and exit as quickly as you can. But this can leave the audience feeling as if your speech has been inconclusive. Instead, slow down, keep your voice strong, keep looking at your listeners, and end with an open-handed 'It is your turn now' gesture and a smile. This way, you are not only signalling that you are about to finish speaking; you are not only signalling that you want your audience's attention right to the last word; you are also signalling that you expect a response from your audience – and a positive response at that.

What Can I Learn by Watching Body Language on the Beach?

If you want the time, the opportunity and the leisure to see body language in all its many forms, take a beach holiday. On the beach you will see almost every kind of nonverbal communication there is: individual, groups, crowds; men, women, children; people flirting, bonding, child-rearing. There is much too much to describe – but here are a few interesting patterns to look for.

As people arrive, watch them mark out their 'territory'. They will spread out towels, put up umbrellas, loungers, windbreakers and even tents – all to claim their spot. They will then decide just where the boundaries are – and very often pace them out. On a crowded beach, territory will extend only as far as the edge of the towel, while on a more deserted beach a group might mark out a strip of territory between them and the sea, and guard it by a constant stream of trips to the water's edge. If another group intrudes, the first group will give hostility signals, glancing across, murmuring among themselves, invading in return by letting a ball or a dog 'accidentally' stray into the other group's space.

As people begin to feel comfortable on their territory, they will start to undress. Beaches, in fact, offer the best displays of public nudity you will ever see. You can tell those whose first day it is on the beach not only by their colour, but also by how slowly they disrobe. By two or three days into their holiday they will not only have got their favourite 'territory' but will be happy to take their clothes off within minutes of settling down. You can, incidentally, often tell just which body part – chest, breast, bum, tum or thighs – each sun-worshipper is most insecure about, because it will be the last one he or she reveals.

Because of this partial nudity – and the inhibitions it places on people – you will rarely see full sexual body language on the beach. But, holidays being what they are, you will see lots of romance. So singles will 'display' their best points in the hope of attracting a mate: women will stretch out long legs and toss their hair back; men will broaden their shoulders and show off their physique by swimming and playing beach games.

Already-existing couples will use body language that shows how very close they are, 'matching' or copying each other's posture, spontaneously lying or sitting in the same way. Watch as they put sun tan lotion on each other: the extent to which each partner is happy to spread it and comfortable about receiving it will be a clear indication of just how far their physical relationship has gone!

Couples with families may occasionally be romantic with each other, but their body language is much more likely to be focused around their children. You can tell by looking just which child is the most trouble – The one that parents compulsively watch. Which child is a bit of a loner? – That will be the one playing far away, with her back turned unconcernedly to the family group. Which child is unhappy or a bit unpopular? – The one who clings to his parents, or who plays alone but with constant glances over at the family group.

So, as you lie back in the sun and slap lotion on all over, put down your blockbuster novel for a while and look around. All human body language is there...